IN SEARCH OF THE MISSING

Working with Search and Rescue Dogs

Mick McCarthy
&
Patricia Ahern

MERCIER PRESS
IRISH PUBLISHER – IRISH STORY

MERCIER PRESS

Cork

www.mercierpress.ie

© Mick McCarthy and Patricia Ahern, 2011

ISBN: 978 1 85635 691 6

10 9 8 7 6 5 4 3 2 1

A CIP record for this title is available from the British Library

Printed and bound in the EU.

—◆—

To my father Jack McCarthy,
and my friends Richard Cotter and Betty Flynn

—◆—

Contents

We were rather like the mourners after the funeral: glad to be alive, getting on with our own lives, the memory of Mick held with sadness and regret, yet accepted as an act that happened; one of the risks of our climbing games.

Is there a self-centred selfishness in this attitude? For those of us who are happily married and have children, there must be or we should not have carried on our life of climbing, aware, as we are, of the risks involved.

In our own single-minded drive and love for the mountains, we hope that the fatal accident will never happen to us, are frightened to contemplate the cruel long-lasting sorrow suffered by the widows, parents and children – an endless tunnel that for them must never seem to end.

From *Everest the Hard Way* by Chris Bonington

Foreword

On 3 September 2006, the day before my wedding, I was in Scotland, and oblivious to the tragic events that were happening at home in Cork. Two men went under the water whilst saving the lives of two others who had gotten into trouble. The nation was gripped for a week as a massive search was undertaken for them. Eventually, their bodies were found.

Mark and I returned home after a thirty-two-hour journey – partly due to delayed flights and missed connections – but still grinning from ear to ear in our post-honeymoon daze. On our way home, we picked up Kram, our collie. I had rescued him eighteen months before from the grounds of a hospital, and had missed him for the three weeks we'd been away. The next day, we called into our neighbours to tell them about our trip, only to be told that one of the men who had been missing was the son of one of my friends. Our neighbours and other friends had felt that it was best not to tell me what had been going on as there would have been nothing I could have done, and they didn't want to spoil our honeymoon.

I wanted to do something as a tribute to my friend's son, and when Mark and I agreed to get another dog, I discovered that there was a dogs' home near where the tragic events had occurred. Having looked at the website (www.westcorkanimals.com), I saw the profile of a collie springer called Chelsea. Given that Mark wanted a springer and I wanted another collie, Chelsea appeared to be the ideal dog. Now, I must point out that, in hindsight, picking a dog over the Internet to match with your existing dog and to join your family is not something that I would ever recommend. Nevertheless, we did it, and – stupidly or not – Chelsea entered our lives and soon became one of the best things to happen to us. However, we went through a lot of stress before we could say that!

Chelsea was in many ways the most difficult kind of dog to adopt. She was nervous and aggressive, and it was clear that her first year of life had not been very good. It took Mark weeks of patience to get close to her, and although she was warmer to me, she would freeze even when I petted her. However, Chelsea was a tribute to my friend's brave son, so there was no way we were giving up on her. We were used to taking Kram everywhere with us as he got on with everyone, but we couldn't do that with Chelsea, and at that stage we didn't know if we would ever be able to. Chelsea was such a frightened dog and we had to start at the beginning with her, just building her trust. Within a couple of months, she was beginning to play fetch, and we could see her relax during the game. Her whole body language would change: her ears and back would relax, and for a while she'd forget she was scared. Chelsea was very good on lead, and she walked perfectly on heel, so at some stage previously someone had loved her enough to train her a little.

Five months later, our pretty but nervous and aggressive

dog was still a handful around strangers, particularly people with hats or walking sticks! Walking the two dogs was difficult and – as I was to learn later – my nervousness was only making things worse. We found ourselves walking in more and more rural settings, trying to avoid meeting other people and dogs.

In August 2007 we decided to attend the Pet Expo in Mallow in the hope of meeting some dog groups that had been advertised on a website. We had run out of ideas on how to bring Chelsea along. In the arena we watched dogs demonstrating agility. Then Mick McCarthy appeared with what was then called the Irish Search and Rescue Dog Association, now called Irish Search Dogs. Mick was charismatic and funny, and at the end of the demo he was available for questions and answers. Mark listened to him for quite some time afterwards, and arranged to bring the dogs to a meeting in Watergrasshill the following week.

The following Sunday, we went to meet everyone, and Mick talked us through how to make our dogs sit beside us and walk on heel. Mick just seemed to understand the different dogs and their temperaments. We were as nervous as hell, and I was so terrified that Chelsea would start barking at people and scare them and embarrass me in front of all these strangers. I was worried that they'd see us as a couple who'd adopted collies and hadn't a clue how much training they needed. In fact, we knew what we were getting into breed-wise, and we loved the long walks and training Kram. He knew 'Fetch my slippers' and 'Tidy up', which meant bringing his toys in from the garden or moving them out of the way of the lawnmower. He just loved to work, and, being a collie, his own intelligence often took over. I remember one night when Mark came in from work and sent Kram off to find his slippers. Kram kept running back into the living-room without them. Mark kept giving the command but still no slippers. Kram got so frustrated that he came over to the sofa, took a slipper off my foot, and threw it at Mark! It turned out Mark's slippers were under a bag and Kram either couldn't find them or didn't think he should move the bag. We fell about laughing.

We needn't have been worried about going along that Sunday; everyone there was so approachable and it helps that Mick can read people as well as dogs. He set about getting me relaxed so that I could help Chelsea relax. As the weeks progressed, Mick showed us how to get the dogs interested in search work and Kram took to it like a duck to water. Suddenly, we were faced with the seriousness of considering training for search work. Mark would be a handler and that was a lot of responsibility. Neither of us knew if we had what it took and how we would react to a casualty or, God forbid, a body. We decided to keep at it and make our minds up if Kram and Mark made the grade.

Chelsea's fear of people became a hurdle to her progressing, but Mick encouraged me to do the training with her to relax her mind and get her thinking. We all had great fun playing 'body' (helpers play the part of the 'body' by hiding and waiting until found by the search dog), and it was amazing to see all the dogs off-lead together on the walks. Everyone in the group knew to ignore Chelsea until she approached them, and this happened soon enough, especially if a ball or food was involved.

Mick taught us how to focus on showing the dogs what to do as opposed to what not to do. Only our own timing hampered his system of dogs learning by association and positive reinforcement. As soon as the penny dropped and we began communicating with them, and thinking of them as dogs, not humans, it all made so much sense.

Soon Kram and Mark were really working well together, and Chelsea was learning to trust people. Chelsea went from barking at my parents when they came to visit, to sitting on my dad's lap and licking his face. On one visit to my parents' house in Waterford, I got up to find Chelsea on the sofa beside my mother, sharing her breakfast. Now, at this point I will say that we don't allow our dogs to beg and we don't feed them from the table. I had wondered why it was that after family visits the dogs took a step backwards. Mum really took to Chelsea's gentle nature. Every time she visited, she'd bring the dogs bones and spoil them rotten. Dad couldn't resist feeding them from the table and teaching them bad habits. Given how Chelsea had been, we allowed it to go on, and were just so happy to finally have a pet as opposed to a problem.

Six months later, Mick asked us during a walk how we had ended up with a dog like Chelsea, and I told him the story. That day, Mick's partner Áine's dog Zak was with us, and Mick pointed to him and said that it was Zak who had indicated where to search for my friend's son, and that his dog Bob was there, too. My heart was pounding in my chest as I realised the full circle that we had come: getting a dog as a tribute to my friend's son had led us to meet the people and dogs who had indicated where to find him. I was speechless, but had to entertain the idea that fate had intervened and this was what we were meant to be doing.

For three hours every Sunday, the dogs and ourselves socialised and trained with like-minded people, and soon enough we were back to taking the dogs everywhere with us: to parties, barbecues and on holidays. Those three hours a week changed our lives and our dogs' lives forever. Little did we know there was more to come.

Eventually, winter came, and the group organised a Tuesday night class in Hop Island Equestrian Centre. Kram and Chelsea became great demonstration dogs, and having gone through and learned so much in teaching them to be great pets, Mark and I began teaching others. Mark and Kram pressed on with their training, and we began going to Kerry and Waterford to expand the terrain for the dogs and handlers. These days out every couple of months were fun, and we'd always finish with a picnic or by going for lunch. We were soon proud to call the group our friends.

In March I contacted the dogs' home to ask if they would like us to foster dogs for them. I felt that we were now in a position to help train some of them so as to make it easier to find homes for them. The dogs' home put me in contact with another centre closer to home, and soon we took in our first foster pup. We only had Dixie a few days before her owners were found, and that was a lovely introduction to fostering. During the next six months, we fostered dogs and puppies, and I discovered that I could manage to re-home them despite my parents' fears that my house would soon be full of dogs. The knowledge gained from Mick and everyone else in Irish Search Dogs meant that even the problem dogs got a greater shot at being re-homed.

We had a fantastic summer with the group and by ourselves out training and hillwalking. Kram's training was taking time, and Mark put in a lot of effort moving on to searching for lost objects, which is known as article searching. One day, when friends of ours lost their dog's collar out walking in rough terrain, we were able to send Kram in and he indicated where it was by barking. In Irish Search Dogs, if you find someone you call in the appropriate emergency services. As time had progressed, we felt less terrified about being in emergencies, and we started to look for ways to increase our training. We felt that it was better to know what to do if you found a casualty. A few of us decided to join the Civil Defence, and in September 2009 we were accepted. What with working full-time, looking after our dogs and foster dogs, and training with Irish Search Dogs and Civil Defence, we were busy, but having the time of our lives.

On 19 September 2009 the local fair was on. I volunteer at it, and we always have an open house for lunch. That year, my sister was over from England, my family was up from Waterford, and my friend Lorna came with her two dogs. Mick and Áine came with their son Jack. I was delighted when I finally introduced Mick and Áine to my mum and dad. Mum had arrived wearing a cowboy hat; she and Mark had a thing for hats, and they'd always try to outdo each other. Thankfully, Chelsea was over her fear of hats by then. My cousin Shannon handled our dogs in the pet-dog show, and Mick and Jack handled their bloodhound Phoebe and won best in show. It was a great day, great weather and great company.

The next day, everything we had trained for came into play as our worst nightmare became a reality. Mum was missing. She had left her house around 5 p.m. Dad rang after 9 p.m., when it got dark, as she still hadn't come home. My mum was scared of the dark, and we all knew something was wrong. Mark, my sister and I, together with Kram and Chelsea, left Cork and headed straight for Waterford. Immediately, we rang Mick and Áine, who talked us through co-ordinating a search. As a family member, I wanted to believe that she would walk in the door any minute, but as the coordinator of a search, I had to cover all possibilities and consider the worst possible outcome. Mark's and my training kicked in. We pushed our emotions aside and geared up. We planned where we would go, based on probability. We sent family members out in cars, and kept in constant contact with them to ascertain where they had been. We began searching around 11 p.m., and as a team were unified. Kram and Mark were amazing to watch. Their connection was so strong despite the fear we were all feeling. An hour passed. We were in constant contact with our friends in Irish Search Dogs, and Mick was preparing to leave Cork to come and help. Time went on, and despite my legs turning to jelly and the pain in our chests and muscles from running, we kept ourselves calm so as to keep Kram working. We knew that if Mark or I broke down it would affect Kram and interfere with his ability to keep searching.

At 1.24 a.m. on 21 September 2009 Kram, Mark, Chelsea and I found my mum. She was not breathing. Mark began CPR – which we had just learned in Civil Defence during the previous week – and I ran to guide in the ambulance personnel. Tragically, my mum never regained consciousness, and was pronounced dead at 5.30 that morning.

Where we got the strength to do what we did that night I will never know. How we managed not to let our emotions get the better of us and how we worked so well as a team throughout it all I will never know. But I do know that three hours on a Sunday morning gave my mum every chance possible and made my family proud. If it wasn't for those three hours every week, then Mum wouldn't have been found so soon and perhaps never at all. I know that the support we got during our search and in the weeks and months afterwards from our family and friends, both in and out of Irish Search Dogs, was wonderful. Now, looking back, I can say that the worst night of my life is also my proudest.

Since that night, Mark and Kram have been training harder, going out several nights a week with the other handlers. On Easter Sunday 2010 they were provisionally qualified as a search dog and handler. I am so proud of what Mark has achieved with Kram.

I urge you if you have two or three hours on a Sunday and a dog that you'd like to train to come along with us or join your local search-dog group and give it a go. We went along for help in socialising our dogs, and look where it has taken us. Not only are our dogs amazing pets, but we are now helping others and have a network of friends and a support system like no other.

We've adopted a new puppy now. Yes, one of our foster puppies. Sorry Mum and Dad, I know I said I wouldn't. Joey is already thriving in his life with us. He's a collie, too, and he loves following Kram when he's working. He looks like he has the potential to take over when Kram retires, and, like the rest of us, Joey loves the three hours on a Sunday.

Suzanne Collings

Prologue

Darkness was setting in when we reached Slieve League. Tensions were running high as fears were now growing that the boy had fallen from the cliffs on the opposite side of the mountain. Searchers had come from everywhere – over a hundred volunteers turned up. A garda superintendent was in charge of co-ordinating the various search teams, which included the Killybegs Coast and Cliff Service Unit, the Shannon Marine Rescue Centre and An Garda Síochána. The Air Corps and the British Royal Navy came and went, flying searchers to and from the scene.

The night was dry but freezing cold. Could the eleven-year-old survive a second night on the mountain in sub-zero conditions? Would the Boy Scout skills he had learned back home in Germany help protect him from the elements? Had he stuck with the Scouts' basic rule of staying put when lost, or had he moved? The youngster's chances were looking slim, but we approached the situation with a very positive attitude, believing that we would find him alive.

We double-checked our gear and prepared to begin our search. A local farmer's teenage son acted as our guide. He showed us the areas already searched, and we combed them again. Then we moved on, scouring the rugged, heathery terrain of the most dangerous mountain in south Donegal.

By now, Neil and I were the only human searchers left

on the mountain. All of the other searchers had been sent home. Eliminating them from the scene would make it easier for the dogs to locate the boy, as their human scent would no longer be present on the mountain. Air-scenting dogs pick up every human scent in a given area, whereas bloodhounds hunt only for the particular scent of the missing person. But there were no bloodhounds available to us. Locating the boy could take hours. There was no time to waste.

Our dogs ranged up to half a mile away from us. Every now and then, when the lamps on their collars shone through the heather, we could pinpoint their location. We knew they were working well. Dogs search best in the dark as they work with their noses, not their eyes, and can detect scents a mile away or up to five miles in certain conditions. Air-scenting dogs work almost as well in daylight, but can occasionally be distracted by other animals or humans. In the dark, they are totally focused.

Hours passed without the slightest hint of progress. We were becoming increasingly concerned. The boy had been missing for nearly thirty-six hours. The treacherous cliffs nagged at our minds, reminding us of their thousand-foot drop into the Atlantic Ocean. But we remained optimistic. Searching with the conviction that the missing person will be found alive helps focus the mind, gives that extra drive, that zip and essential sense of urgency.

At 4.30 a.m. Neil suggested we move over the ridge to the back of the mountain, which was the opposite side to that identified by the Scouts as the location in which they had last seen the youngster. Time was moving fast, and we were aware that the other volunteers would return at first light. If they came back while we were still searching, they would have to wait in the farmyard. Although our dogs are trained to work with multiple handlers at the same time, and will do so ahead of line searchers, there is always a chance that the dogs can be put off by searchers inexperienced in dealing with search dogs. Time-wise, we were under pressure, but we pushed on, determined to find the boy.

Neil and Pepper searched upwards from the bottom. Dex and I worked downwards from the top. After just a further hundred yards, we would be finished with that particular area and switching to yet another part of the mountain. Suddenly, I heard Pepper indicating far below. Neil contacted me on the radio. At that stage, he was about a quarter of a mile below Pepper. Neil suggested I send Dex down to confirm Pepper's indication. Dex made his way downhill, turned left, headed towards Pepper and indicated. Both dogs stood together facing a gully about fifteen feet deep and twenty feet wide, with a sheep fence on top. They cleared the fence, went further in and kept indicating.

Daylight was breaking. Neil and I could see various items in front of us: a guitar, pots and a frying pan. We could see no trace of the boy. But the dogs continued to indicate vigorously.

One Boy and His Dogs

I t's strange that we can go through life without really knowing ourselves. Looking back, it's only now I see I've always been a loner. Even from a very early age, I rarely wanted to be in the company of others. Instead, I preferred to roam through the woods and fields with only my dogs by my side. Dogs were always my best friends, and most of my life revolved around them.

My childhood world in the 1950s was Knockraha – a quiet, east Cork village that only came alive on the annual sports day or when Dolly Daly played the accordion at her garden gate. Mam, Dad, Uncle Danny and the eight of us all lived with Nana Gleeson in her two-storey house, which had two rooms downstairs, with a small lean-to, and was situated in a laneway only a stone's throw from the village church. More people must have set foot in Nana's house than in any other house in the village because it had once been a shop and, before that, a British police barracks. One morning, when my mother got a notion to tear down and replace the front-room ceiling, a shower of guns, bayonets and bean tins full of bullets came crashing down. 'A blast from the past,' my grandmother said. 'There's no escaping it.'

And she was right, because the past is always with us. It latches onto us. It moulds us for tomorrow into something we might or might not want to be. When I was young, I never knew what I wanted to be. The question never even crossed my mind. I was cocooned in my own little world of Knockraha, oblivious to any possibilities beyond it. But I sensed I was different. I never belonged to the pack. I was always moving away, out towards the edges and off in the opposite direction.

I was still only a toddler when the Caseys – a warm-hearted couple who lived next door in the parish house – took a shine to me, plucked me from my family, fussed over me like a little prince, and treated me as one of their own. I kept calling in to them, drawn back time and time again by the red, rosy apples stored in a timber box in their hallway. Even before I started school, Mrs Casey would spend hours talking to me, feeding me stories about faraway places I'd never even heard of, and teaching me how to read, and how to make capital letters and small ones on the lines of a copybook. Even then, I was moving away from the pack. I was out of the traps before the rest, and gone.

I hadn't yet reached my fourth birthday when Mr Casey – who was the local schoolmaster – whisked me off to school one morning. Rubbing his hands together with glee, he marched me up to the top of the classroom and teased the other boys: 'Watch Mikey making his letters correctly on the blackboard. And he's only three!' Sometimes in the schoolyard I got a thumping from the older boys for being the teacher's pet. But it was never very serious. It didn't bother me. I was becoming used to being different.

One of my early-morning jobs in school was to bring a bundle of sticks and some coal into the classroom fireplace, which was the only form of heating in the school. After the fire had been lit, the teacher would tell us to stand by our desks and do 'star jumps' in an attempt to warm ourselves up.

Up through primary school, Mick Mackey was my best friend, my idol. He was the boy with a special demeanour about him, who spoke in a very dignified way, the boy who used to make model aeroplanes with paper, paint them, and hang them from his bedroom ceiling with fishing gut. To me, they were masterpieces. And then, suddenly, he was gone, taken off in an ambulance, never again to return to school, and I was lost without him. Mick was one of the unlucky ones who contracted polio, a disease that plagued Irish children in the mid-1950s but about which I had no understanding at the time. And nobody explained it to me. I missed him a lot, and spent hours sitting alone and crying my eyes out in a shed at the back of Donoghues' pub. I didn't hear of Mick again until years later when someone mentioned that he was working in Dublin as an engineer.

It was around the time of Mick's disappearance that I started to wander off down through the fields and into the glen with my springer spaniel Jessie. I sat there for hours just talking to Jessie. Even when it was wet and windy, I went off with her. I'd sit with my back to a tree or to the wall of a house in the village, and feel the shivers run up my spine. Somehow, it gave me a buzz.

Each morning, Jessie walked me to school, along with my brothers and sisters. She would be waiting at the school door when we came out at lunch time, and again in the evening, to shepherd us safely home.

In the village, I sometimes played with Tommy Maher and Martin Lynch – boys of my own age. But being shy and a loner at heart, I spent most of the time on my own. At home, we didn't have a television. Staying inside and getting under Nana's feet while my parents were out working was never an option. But that was fine for Jessie and me because the days were never long enough for us.

In all our wanderings, I dared not go too far outside the village. I was too scared. The adults had me frightened out of my wits, spinning high tales about wailing banshees and the bogey man, who was always in hiding, waiting for his chance to snatch children away from their families. They warned me about all the eerie sounds around, like echoes and bird chirping, saying they belonged to the ghosts, who always appeared when children ventured too far away from home. They told me to stay well clear of the Fairy Rock in the glen, and never to swim in the river because the big black hole would suck me down. While I believed all that the adults told me, I pushed their warnings to the back of my mind and scuttled off with Jessie to the countryside to play. But I always kept well within my boundaries.

One of my favourite haunts became the riverbank, where I gathered reeds, pressed them between my fingers, and blew with all my might to make a magical, musical sound, just as I often did at home with a comb and paper. I paddled, caught tiny fish with my jam jar, and tightly twisted the lid to keep them in. I rummaged for the flattest stones to skim through the water, or I threw in the rounded ones as far as I could for Jessie to chase.

Late afternoon on a sunny summer's evening was the best time of all. The water was at its warmest then, and Jessie and I crossed from one side of the river to the other. I held onto the branches of heavy old tree trunks, which made a stable bridge across the water, and I hopped from one tree trunk to the next, with Jessie jumping along behind me. Other days, we spent hours hunting rabbits, wading our way through high-grassed fields, bushes, briars and ditches. Sometimes, we sniffed for the scents of other animals or we searched for their tracks. The tracks of the fox, the weasel or the badger, I learned them all from my father. If a big, droopy tree took my fancy, I took out my penknife and carved my initials and the year on it. I promised Jessie that the engraving would still be there when I'd be an old, cranky, toothless man with white hair and a walking stick.

One of my daily chores was to go with my older sister Mary to collect a bucket of milk from Pádraig Dennehy, a local farmer, who always had great time for me. He might let me milk a cow or even ride bareback on one of his horses. Racing through the fields with Jessie running alongside, I felt as free as the wind, like one of those Travellers who galloped through the village on a rare occasion, wild and reckless, and then disappeared from reality, or like one of my classmates, who attended the riding school in Glanmire and often rode his pony from the riding centre in Brooklodge to Knockraha, then all the way back again.

As we had no running water in the house, I was always up and down to the pump, filling two buckets of water at a time and then drawing them back to Nana, who seemed to be forever washing and scrubbing all around her. Sometimes, I thinned beet with my mother and my brother Dan. My mother tied potato sacks around our knees, and told one of us to go to the start of the drill and the other halfway along. We had to keep nine inches between each little plant, and clear away all the excess plants and weeds. My mother thinned two drills at the same time – one with her left hand and one with her right – and could thin two drills in the time it took the two of us together to thin one. Woe betide us if we didn't clean and thin our drill properly! Some farmers' wives would bring us a large churn of tea and sandwiches, but Dan and I never got a penny for our work – my mother kept it all.

Often, Mrs Peter – as she was known locally – let me serve in her shop. I raised myself up on my toes, with my eyes barely able to see over the countertop, and put my number skills to good use by totting up the customer's bill on a piece of paper, while at the same time eyeing up all of the mouth-watering temptations around me, my favourites being sherbets with sticky lollipops, and paper-wrapped, square-shaped toffees.

If I happened to wander into the village post office, Mrs Long, the postmistress, scurried off to her kitchen to fetch me a huge slice of fresh, thickly buttered white bread coated in big, glistening grains of crunchy sugar and cut up into little fingers, like soldiers.

In the evenings, I often cycled miles to accompany my mother home from working on the farms, or I hung around the village with Jessie, dangling my legs from a high wall, waiting to catch the first glimpse of my father returning from the quarry. If the curtains of John Daly's front room were slightly ajar, I stood with my nose pressed against the window and my hands at either side of my forehead, peeping in at the only television in the village, hoping to see one of my favourite programmes, like *Mr Ed*, an American comedy about a sharp, palomino talking horse, who spoke only to his owner, Wilbur Post, and who had a knack for stirring up trouble. Sometimes, the screen showed only jumping, fuzzy lines, and I waited impatiently as John twiddled with the buttons at the back of the television, trying in vain to restore the picture. John worked in the Electricity Supply Board, and had erected a giant of a pole in his garden to receive the BBC. Back then, RTÉ had not even started.

On moonlit nights, I ran with Jessie to the nearest field and stretched out under the sky, scanning my eyes across the heavens for all the different groups of stars, and excitedly shouting their names aloud: the Seven Sisters, the Plough, the Milky Way – I knew them all from my father. On a night when I could see only one star in the sky, I made a silent wish. There was a time when I felt sad that it was all alone. I wondered where all the other stars had gone. But then I decided it was better off on its own. It had the whole, vast sky to itself. It could wander wherever it wanted to go. Nothing was in its way.

It was only natural that I should be close to nature and animals. It was in my genes, planted in the past just like the ammunition in Nana's house. It went way back to a time when my great-grandfather trained horses for the local point-to-point races, or when my father patiently carved an exact wooden replica of a Grand National winner and jockey, having carefully taken the measurements from a newspaper photograph, or when he hunted and ferreted as a boy in his native Ballymacandrick in east Cork.

My father had a way with dogs. When he read the paper in the shed or back garden, they quickly gathered at his feet. And the minute he got up, they followed him without ever a word being spoken. 'Don't talk too much to the dogs, Mikey', he advised me. 'And then they'll trust you more.'

My youngest brother Gerard was just like my father when it came to dogs. In Riverstown, where we moved later, Ger would only have to walk out the gate of the house with his terrier, give a whistle, and, as if by magic, several other dogs would appear and follow him as he went on his daily walk through the local woods and fields. My father got a great kick out of it. 'Mikey! Watch what happens next', he'd call to me. 'Gerard's after whistling.' On arriving back, Ger would saunter in through the gate, and, without a word from him, the dogs would scatter off home.

My brother Dan was different. He hung around with dogs but had no understanding of them. When my father bought a Labrador he saw advertised in the paper, Dan started taking the dog for long walks. One scorching day, he took him into a field near a stream. He stayed there for hours basking in the sun and smoking his cigarettes, and because the dog was too hot, he began to growl over him. When they went home, Dan convinced my mother that the dog was dangerous. Dan was my mother's pet, and she always gave him what he wanted. Nobody dared cross her, least of all my father, who was a silent man. In our house, my mother was a matriarchal figure, and she made all the decisions without ever consulting anyone else. Nobody ever questioned her or argued with what she had said. When she told my father that the Labrador had to go, he went off straight away, without the slightest hint of protest, and sold the dog for £10.

As a child, everything I knew about nature and animals I learned from my father. At the annual sports day in a local field, I watched him set up a pulley system for the dog racing, using an old bicycle, a few hundred yards of twine and a stuffed rabbit skin. Many days, Jessie and I hunted with him, along with his ferret and dogs. When we found a rabbit warren, we made a big circle around it with a net. Then my father put the ferret inside to drive out the rabbits. Sometimes, the ferret stayed down the rabbit hole, and we'd have to go back days later to dig it out. My father had a line of rabbit snares running at intervals down through the fields towards the glen, and each evening he'd take me with him to collect the snared rabbits. We'd put the rabbits into potato sacks and bring them home, where my grandmother would gut and clean them. With their back legs interlaced, they were left hanging in rows from the back-kitchen ceiling until Ger Connell, a local collector, called to take them to the market ten miles away. My mother got a shilling and sixpence for each rabbit – a price that had doubled by the time they reached the market. In those days, it was all about survival.

Although I didn't know it then, hunting trips with my father would form the basis for my work in search and rescue, the main difference being that I would search for humans. The basics were the same. Once the hunting animals made the find, they were rewarded with food or play. Of course, for me back then it was only a game, a sport to enjoy, with Jessie tagging along beside me.

Like most children of my era, I was often shielded from the truth. When there was no sign of Jessie one day after school, Nana never told me she had died but said she had simply gone away. I ran breathlessly to Donoghues' backyard, in through the woods and down to the glen, yelling her name at the top of my voice. I combed the riverbank and fields, and watched for her return at every corner. Then we moved away, and I left my innocence behind. Our new home was a semi-detached council house in Riverstown, a village nearer Cork city. And, boy, did I get the biggest culture shock of my young life. There were gangs of youngsters everywhere. They pelted each other with stones at every chance. And although some were only my own age, they were all much more advanced.

Riverstown was a much bigger area than Knockraha, and I now felt like the stranger up from the country. I was reluctant to step outside my own front door for fear of a thumping. And there wasn't an ounce of sympathy coming from my mother, who was a hard, robust woman. Once, she had taken part in a scuffle on a hurling pitch at White's Cross and nearly left an opposing player for dead after he hit a player from our local team, who happened to be the son of one of her friends. But without ever making a fuss, my father threw me a lifeline. He knew all the old men in Riverstown from talking to them as they passed up and down with their dogs, and some were members of the Riverstown Foot Beagles. Dexter, a beautiful, three-month-old liver-

and-white beagle came into my life when two club members brought him to our door, asked me to rear him, and invited me along to the club. My heart jumped for joy, and straight away I forgot about everything else. Dexter was my survival kit, and we became great friends.

Going off with the hunting pack to a meet on a Sunday morning was exhilarating. I hurried after the dogs, watching their every twist and turn, delighting in their chase and bursting with pride as Dexter scampered along with the rest. The day we travelled to Tallow for a joint meet was the best day of all as I had never before been so far from home. For ages after, I ranted and raved about the road trip, and repeated word for word the doggy conversations of the day. I entertained my father, imitating the strange accent of the Tallow people and rattling off the names of the Tallow dogs.

In the early days, I never saw a kill with the pack as it wasn't always possible to keep up with the hunt. Then, months after joining, I witnessed one for the first time. When I was younger, I never had any qualms about a kill carried out by hunting, dazzling or ferreting. As a teenager, it affected me differently: I shook with shock as I saw a hare being torn asunder by the pack of beagles. Even though the kill was very fast, I was upset for a long time afterwards. I never again attended a meet.

My world fell apart when I came home one day to find Dexter gone, retrieved by the club. The pain I had felt when Mick Mackey disappeared from my life returned. For weeks after, I would climb over the walls of the hunt kennels and sit for hours beside the dogs just to be near them.

One winter's night, my father walked in with a big grin on his face and a pup for me warmly tucked under his coat. Without a second glance, I rejected him. By then, I had made up my mind that I would no longer seek solace in dogs or nature. This time, I would deal with the pain differently. I joined a local boxing club, punched out all my frustration in the ring, and used up all my energy prancing around like Muhammad Ali. I started guitar lessons, all paid for by my older sister Mary, who was now working in a local hospital. I practised with determination and obsession, convinced I was the next Elvis. I started playing in local concerts with Johnny Dwyer, a local guitar player who could play by ear, and I became part of the local hurling and football teams, much to the annoyance of my mother, who was now giving out, complaining that I should be spending more time at home.

Attending secondary school in the city and doing my homework kept me busy, too. While I had won scholarships to several schools, I soon turned my back on education when I became one of the many Irish schoolchildren abused by religious orders in the 1960s. One particular brother at the secondary school in Sullivan's Quay had been mentally torturing me for some time – ever since he spotted I was having difficulty with the Irish language. To escape him, I often pretended to my mother that I had a bad pain in my side, so much so that the doctor concluded that if I complained one more time I should have my appendix removed. The abuse continued. On the day the brother belted me around the head with a leather strap, I punched him under the jaw and floored him. The brother in the classroom next door paraded me up to the head brother, who gave me a week's suspension on the spot.

By then, I had been in the school only four or five months. Not having the guts to tell my mother, I put on another convincing act of being doubled up with pain. She called an ambulance. I was rushed off to hospital, and operated on the following morning. When I woke up after the operation, I found a nun staring down at me; 'Michael McCarthy, I think you were codding us!' she said, pointing her finger at me. By now, I had metal clips inserted and a fine scar that would last me a lifetime. 'Well?' she asked, raising her brow and waiting for my reply. I told her the truth there and then.

When my mother learned about the abuse, she was so shocked that she made up her mind not to send me back to school. She arranged for me to start full-time work in Haughton's timber yard in Riverstown. I was out on the margins again, gone from my own age group and working with men as old as my father. Working in the timber yard was hard labour for a boy of my age. After twelve tough months of lugging around heavy timber, I developed a big lump on my shoulder. That was my wake-up call. Within days, I was back studying for my Group Certificate at a different school in the city, and into my old routine of homework, boxing and the guitar. Sometimes at night, while studying or strumming my guitar, I'd notice my father peering at me over the top of his newspaper. Deep down, I knew he was wondering just how long more it would take before I'd open my heart and get back on track with the dogs.

Between the Gigs and the Reels

The music scene in Ireland in the 1960s was buzzing, and I was in the thick of it, playing with bands up and down the country, and going along to gigs on my Suzuki Twin motorbike. Most of the time, I was surrounded by people. Yet I rarely felt part of the group. I was still the shy, awkward, introverted country boy, lingering on the outside, looking in. But music had taken over my life. I'd become obsessed with it, just as I would later become obsessed with the dogs.

When I started a secretarial course after my Inter Cert, I soon became the last male standing in a class full of sixteen-year-old girls. All the other lads had absconded, having had their fill of doodling strokes on a shorthand notebook, tracing the pages of Mr Gregg's yellow-cover book, and being corrected every time they slumped at the typewriter. As for me, I was in for the long haul, scared as I was of my female classmates, afraid to even glance in their direction, knowing I'd blush all over if I as much as saluted them. But I'd taken to the shorthand and typing like a duck to water, and there was no getting rid of me without my certificates in hand. Determined to make myself oblivious to all the loveliness around me, I focused on the task ahead. Sitting upright at the top of the typewriting class, I stared straight in front, kept my eyes firmly glued to the wall chart, and pounded away at my typewriter until it made a rhythm all of its own. I typed with precision and speed, wasting no time at all in rolling in crisp, white sheets of paper, setting tabs, or changing red-and-black ribbons.

Before every shorthand class, I loosened up my right hand, squiggling line after line of intertwining circles, one row towards the right of the page and the next to the left. Outside of the class, I even began to think in shorthand. I wrote words, phrases, brief forms and sentences in my head. Shorthand became my new language, a secret code, a silent tongue, which suited me. In no time at all, my speeds had gone through the roof. I was way ahead of the girls, top of the class, and ready to re-enter the world of full-time work.

My first job was in the office of a prominent hardware company based in Cork city. I hated being cooped up in an office with six girls who were all much older and wiser than me. My mother took pity on me, and after my nine weeks of hell took me along for an interview with a friend of a friend who was the manager of another hardware company. Because I was a country boy, I was hired straight away, and began my career as a sales assistant with Munster Glass, a Cork city-centre-based firm, where I still work today.

Though they were regular customers, I always shuddered at the sight of some of the builders. They were tough, hard men, and always called me Tasher, because of my moustache. They'd march right up to the counter waving their lists of material and shout, 'Hey, Tasher – I want this straight away!' They appeared threatening, as if they were going to give me a rough ride. But they never did, not once in all of my forty-two years of service. Behind the tough façade, they were all good, decent blokes.

But it was the girls in the office who singled me out for some special treatment, recognising me for what I was: a greenhorn in from the country and an easy target for some fun. At the end of the morning tea break, the boss would sometimes tell me to call the girls out from the canteen if they had stayed there over the time. I'd knock gently on the door, stick in my beetroot head, and meekly say, 'I'm sorry but the boss told me to tell you to come out.' One morning, one of them said to me, 'If you ever stick your cheeky little face in here again, we'll strip you to the bone!' And not long after, they did. They threw my clothes out the window, pushed me out the door for the rest of my workmates to see, and gloated, 'Now let that be a lesson to you!'

Shortly after starting with the glass company, I began a series of night classes, first to sit my Leaving Cert and later to take other tests, including accountancy exams.

Although my job at Munster Glass was reasonably well paid, I had little to show for it. My mother still had many mouths to feed, and she was calling the shots. Every payday, I obediently handed her my pay packet, unopened. She gave me back five shillings – just about enough for me to indulge in the hobby which warmed my heart and touched my soul: music. Since I first began plucking away at a guitar, the music world had sucked me in, and my interest in dogs lay dormant, for a while at least. By the time I joined Munster Glass as a sixteen-year-old, I could read crotchets, quavers and semibreves with ease, and play the guitar, piano, piano accordion, violin and mandolin to a standard good enough for public performance. Already playing part-time on the music circuit, I was eager to take on more stints and ready to grasp any breaks to come my way.

Getting gigs was easy. Newspapers were dotted with advertisements for musicians to audition, join bands or simply fill in for a night. Being versatile and able to read music – which was a rarity then – was a passport to work. And the gigs poured in. At first, transport to the venues posed a problem. But then my mother agreed to go guarantor for a Suzuki Twin and I was made! At the time, a guy of my age wouldn't be seen dead on a Honda, but a Suzuki – now that was upmarket! With my amplifier and guitar covered in plastic and tightly strapped to the front and rear of the bike, I was ready to hit the road and raring to go.

The range of venues and opportunities was endless. I played at weddings and cabarets, in pubs, ballrooms and concert halls. I strummed along in the orchestra pit at the Cork Opera House, and sweated it out at sessions with *céilí* bands. Usually, the *céilí* took place in a community hall or school, like the Inniscarra hall or the schoolhouse in Eyeries in west Cork. Any number of musicians might turn up, as it was all very casual. A session could end up having three drummers or four or five accordion players. Some nights, so many musicians arrived there wasn't enough money to pay everyone. As I was usually the youngest taking part, I often got the short straw and came away with no money at all. Once, I remember playing at a schoolhouse in Kealkil, in west Cork. No room was big enough to cope with the crowd, so the musicians played in one room and everyone else danced to the music in the room next door.

For a time, I gigged as a guitarist with a local band, and did a six-month stint with a professional showband from up the country. I appeared on televised pop-chart and music shows, much to the annoyance of my employer, who quite rightly began to wonder how I could possibly put in a decent day's work if I was up half the night! He warned me that playing in the bands was bound to come against me at some stage, maybe even put my job on the line. But I paid no heed, and would arrive into work in the mornings straight from a gig the night before, often from places as far away as Galway.

Of all the venues, the ballroom was my favourite. On stage part of me was on cloud nine as we belted out all the latest chart songs, from Tom Jones' 'Green Green Grass Of Home' to The Beatles' 'All You Need Is Love'. At the same time, I was scared out of my wits and overwhelmed by the whole situation. While playing, I never dared raise my head or even look at the crowd. I stayed at the back of the stage, and kept my head down – so much so that nobody could possibly recognise me.

In those days, all the single girls stood together at one side of the ballroom. Many of them wore black velvet hairbands, a testimony to Johnny McEvoy's huge hit, 'Black Velvet Band'. The guys came along and invited them onto the floor. It was like a stampede. If a girl refused to dance, the guys often retaliated with comments like, 'You should have brought your knitting' or 'What are you waiting for – the resurrection?' But despite any cheeky remarks, it was a fun night out for everyone. And the energy was palpable as we got the crowd swinging their hands in the air to hits like 'Simon Says' or twisting to 'The Hucklebuck'.

After the shows, the girls and guys crowded excitedly in front of the stage. Waving their multicoloured autograph books high above them, they scrambled to meet the band. That was when I made myself scarce. I was too shy and couldn't cope. While the rest of the lads lapped up the adulation, I busied myself stripping down the band's gear, packing it and loading it onto the van. I was the odd man out. But that never frightened me away. Music had me hooked, and it consumed my life even when I wasn't on stage. Every morning, I woke up to an array of stars peering down at me: The Beatles, Joe Dolan, Brendan Bowyer, Elvis, Cliff, The Tremeloes, Petula Clark, The Monkees and Sandie Shaw – they were all plastered on my bedroom walls. Gazing up in awe at these superstars, I studied the hairstyles and costumes of the guys, and wavered between becoming a Davy Jones or Paul McCartney lookalike.

Working in the city centre meant the music industry was right on my doorstep. At lunch hour, I hurried off to Shanahan's music shop in Oliver Plunkett Street. I flicked through the new singles and LPs. I examined every detail of album covers, and compared record labels. At the time, very few youngsters of my age were buying records. Instead, they swapped around their music as many had reel-to-reel tape recorders.

I became a daily visitor to Crowley's music shop on Merchants Quay, where Mr Long danced attendance on me and on all the other young musicians. He was the old-style music gent. With his white hair and bow tie, he looked as if he belonged to another era. His son Denis was another culture lover, and well known for his involvement in the arts world. Then, when Mr Long retired, Paul Byrne stepped in. He was a great musician, and highly respected by all of the young musician customers. Paul was Ireland's Hank Marvin of The Shadows, and was known to all and sundry as Hank. Everyone greatly valued his opinion and sought his advice before making any purchase. But Crowley's always had notable assistants – top-class people, only the best. My time spent there at lunch hour was precious, and I used it well, examining instruments, scanning music sheets or checking out notices on upcoming events and second-hand instruments for sale.

Buying *Spotlight* magazine in Eason's became one of the highlights of my week. I was impatient for all the latest on the music scene in Ireland and across the globe, keen to get my hands on the words of one more new song, and to collect yet another pop poster to adorn my wall. I stashed the magazines in the attic, stacks upon stacks of them, going back to the very first issue in April 1963 when *Spotlight* started as a monthly publication, then on to 1967 when it became a weekly issue. Over the years, the magazine changed its name, first to *New Spotlight* and later to *Starlight*. I had them all, and kept them for decades, a treasured collection and a prized possession.

At the same time, I also gathered music sheets going back to 1968 and music books as far back as 1966. On the front of each of them I carefully wrote my name and the date, a clear reminder to any borrower that they were mine and should be returned. While I was more than happy to share, I gave nothing away for keeps. I was an out-and-out hoarder and wanted all the pieces of the jigsaw in order, slotted together, fully intact. In later years, I changed from collecting music material to gathering doggy books, magazines, videos and DVDs – in fact, anything I could lay my hands on to increase my knowledge of dogs.

If I was at home, no matter what I was doing, the radio was always buzzing away in the background. I waited with bated breath for the chart shows, eager to find out if 'I'm a Believer' could hang on as number one for four weeks in a row or if the Sinatras' 'Somethin' Stupid' would be blown off the top spot by the Eurovision winner 'Puppet on a String'. And I never ever went to sleep without the jingles of Radio Luxembourg ringing in my ears.

Some nights, I called to my friend John O'Connor, a saxophone player who worked full-time as a groom in a riding school in Glanmire owned by a woman called Mrs Magner. John had cardboard boxes of demo discs, all sent to him by his employer's cousin, who was a record producer in England. We'd spend hours in his room, which overlooked the stables, watching the horses below, listening to the demos, and rummaging through 78s or 45s, always spoiled for choice. These demos had never been intended for release but were printed solely to allow well-known singers and bands to select songs they wanted to record. Some of the material on the demos was amazing. One of the regular singers happened to be a session singer named Gerry Dorsey, who later became famous as Engelbert Humperdinck. Having listened to the demos for hours, we might head off on John's motorbike to the Elm Tree bar in Glounthaune, where I might have a rum and blackcurrant, or in to Mattie Kiely's chipper in the city for fish and chips, followed by an ice-cream cone from Keane's shop in Patrick Street, often not touching down at home until midnight.

Other nights, I travelled miles to gigs just to watch and listen. If the gig happened to be in a dance hall, I perched myself against a pillar for the night, focused on the band and savoured the atmosphere. I marvelled at the brilliance of certain lead singers, such as the legendary Joe Dolan, who had the girls swooning the minute he hopped on stage, or Dickie Rock, who had the crowds screaming 'Spit on me Dickie!' I listened attentively to the musicians, concentrating on every aspect of their performance, from arrangements to acoustics, harmony and amplification.

I had never led the life of a normal teenager, partly because I hated smoking and drinking. Once, over a twelve-month period, I did drink, but a female drummer in the band I was with at the time laid down the law that none of us could drink if we wanted to play in the band. After that, I gave up the booze and turned against it completely.

From the time I started at Munster Glass until the age of twenty-one, I had been constantly on the go, keeping down a full-time job, gigging, practising music, attending night classes and studying. For every minute of every waking hour, I had been busy – a trend I continued later with the dogs. Yet while I was always out and about in the midst of people, I was rarely actually socialising. And I certainly wasn't making any effort to find myself a girlfriend.

In that era of the showbands, most young people met their partners in dance halls. As I never had the nerve to ask a girl out to dance, romance remained totally beyond my reach. Then, unexpectedly, it appeared. One of my mates – an Irish and international basketball player – worked with me at Munster Glass as a glass-cutter. Because of his high profile, he was often invited to functions all over Ireland and he regularly asked me along for company. Most of the gatherings were male-only affairs, so we rarely met girls. On one very wet, cold night, he invited me to go along with him as he had two free passes to Garry's Inn in Coburg Street, a popular Cork showband venue. He introduced me to a girl there named Marie, and spent the rest of the night trying to coax me into dancing with her. Eventually, he persuaded me to walk her home. Leaving my motorbike behind, Marie and I headed off on foot in the pouring rain, uphill towards the North Cathedral and beyond. I couldn't believe I was walking a girl home. I became tongue-tied. But it didn't matter. Marie was talking at the rate of a mile a minute, and I probably couldn't have got a word in edgeways even if I had wanted to. Once we reached her door, she said, 'This is my house.'

'Well, goodnight, so,' I timidly replied. Then I turned on my heels and was gone like a bullet.

When I tried to make my way back down to the city, I got lost. I must have looked some sight, walking around in circles in the lashing rain and wearing my motorbike helmet. After what seemed like two hours, I finally found Coburg

Street, hopped on my bike and headed for home. I wasn't aware of it then, but in meeting Marie I had also found my wife-to-be. On the night before our wedding, I stripped all the pop posters from my bedroom walls and handed up my pay packet to my mother for the last time. I was closing the door on an old way of life and beginning a new.

Stepping Stones

S ometimes, the smallest of decisions can take us off in a direction we never planned to go and from which there may be no return. From my teenage years to my early twenties, music had dominated my life. One day, a colleague at the glass company announced he had a black, six-month-old cocker spaniel for sale. On an impulse, I made up my mind to buy him, much to the surprise of Marie, who quickly reminded me that we had no proper place for a pup in our new home in the city.

I confined him to the kitchen and hoped for the best. In only a matter of days, I knew I was in big trouble when I saw that he had chewed off the kitchen window sills and all the legs of the table. Luckily, I found a woman who wanted a replacement for her old dog, and she gave him a good home. But by then, my love for dogs had been reignited, and I was soon on the lookout for another family pet.

Next came Cleo, a female Doberman pup. We converted the area under the stairs for her, and this became her surveillance base for all the comings and goings of the house. One day, when Marie was at home alone, some Travellers came begging. By now, this particular pair had become regular callers. On the advice of a friend, Marie decided it was time to put an end to their calls. When she declined to give them anything, they got very annoyed and refused to leave. Marie became anxious. She tried to close the door but the women pushed it hard against her and knocked her back into the hallway. Marie screamed for Cleo. She came charging out from under the stairs and jumped aggressively at the pair. They ran for their lives, never to be seen again. But that wasn't Cleo's only claim to fame. As I was walking with her through Cork city one evening, some youths surrounded us and refused to let us pass. I gave Cleo her alert command and instantly she leaped at them. Frightened out of their wits, they separated and made way for us to walk by.

Of all the dogs we ever owned, Alla, a black miniature poodle, was the toughest and the best family pet. Named after the Scottish mountain Ben Alla, he arrived as a five-month-old, and straight away made himself at home by cheekily settling into a cosy armchair. When one of my daughters sat down on a chair beside him, he suddenly turned and snapped at her. But despite getting off to a bad start, he soon became a firm family favourite, proving himself highly intelligent and capable of being trained for any purpose. He remained with us for thirteen years.

During that time, we also owned a standard schnauzer, a Weimaraner and a German shepherd named Ben, who was an excellent show and obedience dog. From the word go, we made a great team, and travelled the country together giving demonstrations on obedience, agility and protection. Over the years, I competed in dog shows as well as obedience and agility competitions with several different registered breeds of dog, including poodles, German shepherds, Dobermans, schnauzers, Weimaraners and numerous mixed breeds.

For several years, beginning in 1979, I judged all registered breeds of dogs under Irish Kennel Club rules at dog shows.

Well and truly back in the doggy mode, I was now ready to become more heavily involved in dog training. Around 1982 we moved from our first home at Boherboy in Mayfield back out to the country, to my native Knockraha, where I began a training club, Ortsgruppe Erin's Own (later, this became part of the German Shepherd Working Dog Association). At first, the club was exclusive to German shepherd dogs and through the German Shepherd Association (GSA), founded by Marie and John Buckley in Limerick, we practised the sport of *schutzhund*, which is a German word for 'protection dog' training.

Marie and John's dedication and commitment to the German shepherd dog and the sport of *schutzhund* was unsurpassed. They went on to become two of the most influential people in the world of German shepherd dogs. John was, and still is, one of the most respected show and *schutzhund* judges in the world. When practised properly, *schutzhund* is the best dog sport of all. It has three different aspects: obedience, tracking and protection. As the standard of obedience is very high, only the most controlled and obedient dogs qualify.

Before being allowed to take part in *schutzhund* training, owners and dogs must first qualify in *begeitlinghund*, known as BH, which is a traffic test focusing on sureness and temperament. While training for the BH degree, dogs with suspect temperament, such as aggression or nervousness, are quickly weeded out and prevented from making it through to the *schutzhund* field. For the obedience phase of *schutzhund*, dogs must obey the commands of their handlers to perform a variety of skills, such as heeling at their handlers' side, retrieving and jumping.

In the tracking phase, the dog works on a thirty-foot lead and follows with deep nose (where its nose is scuffing along the ground, searching for the footprints of the tracklayer) a previously laid track that contains a number of the tracklayer's articles. Once an item is found, the dog must lie down or sit until the handler comes alongside and retrieves the article.

For the protection phase, six blinds, or hides, are placed – three on each side – along the sides of the training field, and a person acting as a helper is concealed. The handler and dog begin walking down the centre of the training field. Then, on command from the handler, the dog searches each blind, left and right, until he or she finds the helper, who is dressed in a padded suit and sleeve. The helper stays motionless while the dog sits and barks in front of them. This is called 'stand off'. To pass the protection phase, a number of scenarios must be completed successfully by the dog and handler, all of which involve total control of the dog by the handler.

A handler can achieve a number of different *schutzhund* degrees. These range from SchA to Sch3, which is the highest degree available. For many years, Ireland has been sending dog teams to compete in the World Schutzhund Championships. In 2005 the Irish achieved seventh place in the world in overall scores, and first place in the world in tracking. While most other sporting achievements are acknowledged by both the government and the public, this great feat was never recognised, yet to dog owners this is the ultimate in dog training.

Because of my involvement with the sport of *schutzhund*, particularly the tracking phase, I began to consider the possibility of using our dogs for search-and-rescue work. At this stage, I knew very little about search-and-rescue training with dogs other than what I had read. I founded the Cork Area Search and Rescue Dog Association (CSARDA) in 1983, through which I was able to invite all dog owners and their dogs – whether thoroughbred or mixed breed – to training. Having leased some land, we set up agility equipment, a show ring and a protection area.

However, I wanted to take *schutzhund* tracking a little further, into more real-life situations. The other two CSARDA club members, Gerry Brennan from Castletownbere and Don Murphy from Cork city, teamed up with me, and we began training our dogs in search and rescue. When, in my naivety, I considered our dogs to be of practical use in real-life scenarios, I contacted Con Moriarty of the Kerry Mountain Rescue Team. Con showed great enthusiasm about our dogs, and advised me to ring Neil Powell, a search-dog handler from Northern Ireland. Neil was the leader of the Mourne Mountain Rescue Team and was responsible for introducing air-scenting dogs to Northern Ireland in the mid-1970s. He used his dog Pepper regularly in call-outs, not only in Ireland but also in Scotland. In the years to come, he became the first search-dog handler in the world to train dogs to detect counterfeit DVDs, and trained the first ever water-search dog in the United Kingdom. Initially, Neil had trained under Hamish MacInnes, the renowned Scottish mountaineer who developed modern mountain rescue in Scotland, who designed the first all-metal ice axe and the MacInnes stretcher – which is used in rescue operations worldwide – and who founded the Search and Rescue Dog Association. Hamish was first inspired to train dogs when he went to Switzerland and saw rescue dogs working there in the snow. On his return to Scotland, he began training German shepherds for avalanche work.

Neil agreed to visit us, and arrived at our training grounds. Being a schoolteacher, he had an air of authority about him without it being obvious. He soon put us straight. Neil told us that tracking dogs are of little use in real-life searches, whereas air-scenting dogs can work solely by air scent and rapidly get on the trail of a missing person. They can pick up a scent 120 feet under water, and cover as much ground in one hour as ten people can in four hours. Air-scenting dogs work with their heads up all the time. But tracking dogs work with their noses down, which is much harder and more tiring for a dog.

To show us what was needed, Neil gave a short demonstration with his air-scenting dog. Then he tested some of our dogs to check their suitability as air-scenting dogs. He explained that as well as training a dog, search-dog handlers had to be members of a recognised mountain-rescue team, have a current mountain-rescue first-aid certificate, be extremely proficient at reading a map and compass, and be competent with a rope and harness. When I had assimilated all this information, I realised I knew next to nothing about serious dog training. I had been truly knocked off my pedestal. There was I thinking I knew everything about dog training and that search training would be a doddle to me. What an idiot!

After Neil's visit, I quickly concluded that Kennel Club obedience, agility, *schutzhund* and all the other facets of sports-dog training only barely touched on a dog's capabilities. I realised that I had only been playing at being a dog trainer, and felt I had to give serious thought to forgetting all about search-dog training. But then Con and Neil convinced me otherwise, and Neil told me that he had been trying for some time to form a national search-dog organisation similar to the one already in existence in Britain. Some months later, in 1987, he invited a group of about ten of us to meet in Laragh, County Wicklow. After a long discussion, we officially formed the voluntary Search and Rescue Dog Association of Ireland, or SARDA Ireland, as we call it today. Our aim was to search for missing persons. A sergeant from the Garda Dog Training Unit in Dublin became our first chairperson and Neil was elected as our training officer. With search-dog teams, it's customary that the training officer rules supreme. This meant that Neil would have full control of the running of the organisation, including qualifications, call-outs, training and contact with other rescue teams in the country.

Having agreed to hold a training weekend in the Wicklow Mountains every six weeks, everyone returned home filled with enthusiasm and eager to begin proper search-dog training. Little did I know what lay before me! While my commitment to SARDA Ireland involved me in search-and-rescue operations and provided me with opportunities to work abroad, it also took a heavy toll on my personal life, especially my marriage.

Lockerbie

A year after SARDA Ireland was launched, a major tragedy in which hundreds were killed shook the very foundations of search-and-rescue organisations. The Lockerbie air disaster occurred on 21 December 1988 when a Pan American World Airway's Boeing 747-121 – named *Clipper Maid of the Seas* – exploded during a transatlantic flight from Heathrow Airport in London to John F. Kennedy Airport in New York. The explosion killed 243 passengers, sixteen crew members and eleven people on the ground in Lockerbie, in south-west Scotland, where huge sections of the plane hit the ground. The deceased came from twenty-one different countries.

Dealing with such a horrendous aftermath stretched search-and-rescue resources to the limit and had a serious impact on search-and-rescue organisations. At the time, SARDA Ireland had only three internationally qualified search dogs: Pepper – a collie belonging to Neil – together with a golden retriever and a bearded collie, both belonging to Vicky and Mitch Cameron, a married couple from Northern Ireland. For a number of years, the three dogs and their handlers had trained regularly with SARDA Scotland. All were experienced mountain rescuers. When the Lockerbie disaster happened, they were summoned to the scene. None of them had ever dealt with the horrors of a plane-crash disaster before.

At least fifty international dogs, including police dogs, took part in the search. As well as having to look for bodies, the dog teams had to search for body parts and debris from the plane. Search dogs are initially trained to search for live bodies, but can quickly switch to a search for various articles simply by having a relevant item put before them and used as their toy for a few minutes.

Neil, Vicky and Mitch spent five days at Lockerbie over the Christmas period searching with the dogs. The horror and awfulness of finding human bodies left its mark on all three of them. Afterwards, Neil commented that his life could really be defined as before and after Lockerbie – it had been that traumatic. Pepper had recovered the remains of sixteen people. Within days of returning from Lockerbie, one of Vicky and Mitch's dogs died, reportedly from inhalation of aviation fuel, which had spread around the area. Later, some of the international search handlers involved in the search, who were extremely traumatised by what they had seen at Lockerbie, retired from their search organisations. Usually, the effect of dealing with such a tragedy might not surface for months afterwards and counselling is essential.

Because of the disaster, new structures came into force. An international search-dog association was set up in Britain: the British Overseas Disaster Unit. Neil and I were founding members, even though we were not British – rescue people have no international boundaries. Phil Haigh was elected as deputy leader with Dave Riley as team leader. Dave was well known in doggy circles, especially in Cumbria, where he acted as an assessor for the official search dog assessments.

Other guys in the disaster unit included a camp manager, paramedics, a dentist, a doctor and a communications manager. Penny Kirby and Jim Greenwood were based in England to act as contacts and to deal with the press. At that stage, we had only six dogs on the team: two in Ireland and four in England. The organisation was willing to fly to any place in the world where dogs could be successfully used to search for people lost in disaster situations, such as flooding, mud slides or earthquakes.

Neil and I hoped that the Irish government might step in and, at the very least, offer us a training area at Collins Barracks in Cork or at Kilworth Camp, near Fermoy, but no such luck. We've since learned through experience that the Irish government will only help out when it's under the spotlight – such as in the later case of a missing German Boy Scout. When the focus of the international media was on Ireland, the government immediately lent a helping hand. A government jet was laid on to fly Neil and me from Cork to Donegal to take part in the search for the German lad. Other than that, we have never been offered any type of help. On the other hand, the British government couldn't do enough for us. It set us up with a training area in Northern Ireland, and we had the Royal Air Force at our beck and call.

Neil and I began to train together in earnest, but then a whole set of new rules came into play following a major mudslide disaster in Afghanistan. The British Overseas Disaster Unit sent two of the team's dogs to Afghanistan to take part in the search for the living and the dead. But while the dogs proved successful in finding dead bodies, they ignored the live ones. After that, an order was issued that every dog on the team should be trained only to look for live bodies. This was impractical for dogs working in Ireland. Our dogs need to be cross-trained as, on average, nine out of ten people found here are deceased. This is primarily because civilian search-dog teams are not called in until one or two weeks after someone is reported missing.

At that stage, I decided to pull back from the disaster unit. I hadn't time to do specialist emergency training. I opted to make Ireland my priority and to stick with the cross-training. I felt I had no choice, as Ireland needed its own search dogs. Vicky and Mitch had already lost one of their dogs, and Neil's dog Pepper had reached old age. The Lockerbie aftermath gave us that final push to qualify our dogs. It underlined the need for us at SARDA Ireland to increase our number of search dogs and search-dog handlers sooner rather than later, and made us more committed than ever to passing the official search dog assessment.

On 31 January 2001 Abdelbaset Ali Mohmed al-Megrahi was convicted of 270 counts of murder for the bombing of Pan Am Flight 103 over Lockerbie. He was sentenced to life imprisonment, with a recommendation that he should serve at least twenty years before being considered for parole. Under Scottish regulations, prisoners can be released on compassionate grounds if they are considered to have only three months or less to live. In 2009 he was freed from jail on compassionate grounds after it was concluded that he would be dead in less than three months from prostate cancer. Megrahi had served less than nine years of his life sentence.

Having been released, the bomber returned to Tripoli and defied the medical prediction.

A Mountain to Climb

From the time SARDA Ireland was founded, search-dog training took up every spare minute of my time. Just as I had been obsessed with music and *schutzhund* training, I now became obsessed with training a dog for search-and-rescue work. Every hour outside of work was spent with the dogs. I trained seven days a week, including every Christmas day and all holidays.

I am ashamed to admit it, but I put my wife and family totally to one side. Unless they were training with me, they hardly saw me. Such neglect caused great difficulty at home, but I wasn't willing to listen to reason. Time and time again, I promised that as soon as I had qualified one search-and-rescue dog, I would ease back a little. It never came to be. Now, I realise I was on a roller coaster, and I didn't want to get off. To put it simply, it was an ego trip, a total obsession. I didn't care. I just wanted to keep going.

To make matters worse, doggy friends and fellow club members constantly doubted my ability to succeed. Often, they told me I would never qualify a dog for search-and-rescue work. Being as stubborn as I am, this was like showing a red rag to a bull. As friends who know me well will testify, if I am told I will not succeed, especially where dogs are concerned, I will go all out to prove that I can. In my mind, there was one, and only one, way to succeed, and that meant perfect practice. Once, I came across a book on *schutzhund* which stated, 'Practice does not make perfect. It's perfect practice that makes perfect.' This became my mantra.

All through this time, Don was with me. He was caught up in the training as much as I was, but, being a single man, it didn't affect his home life as much as it did mine. As well as becoming dog trainers, we had to become members of a recognised mountain rescue team, obtain a current mountain-rescue first-aid certificate, be extremely proficient in compass work and reading a map, and be competent with a rope and harness. Knowing that we had a long, tough road ahead, we lined up everyone we knew to help.

Our families came up trumps. We depended heavily on them, especially to act as 'bodies'. Without bodies, or helpers, training is impossible, as several people are needed to train a dog. Normally, a body has to hide in the woods or mountains in all types of weather and wait until found by the search dog. This type of search-dog training is based on air scenting, which means that a dog will find all humans in a particular area, whether they are the missing persons or 'innocent' hillwalkers. When innocent walkers are 'found', the handler will explain the situation and ask them to leave the area of the search. Sometimes, these walkers may have seen or found evidence of the missing person, such as a backpack. If they are experienced hillwalkers, they may even help in the search.

When found, the bodies must reward the dogs with food or play, using a ball or some other toy. The dogs then learn to associate the toys with the find, until eventually the dogs believe that in all searches they are, in fact, looking for their toys. For that reason, the toy must always be produced at the point of the find. The bodies can make or break the dogs. Their input in training is vital, especially their reaction on being found, how they play with the dogs, and how they build up a relationship with them. Our usual bodies included my wife Marie, my sister Celine, as well as Don's brothers, Declan and Tom. And all of them often suffered absolute torture in an effort to help us train our dogs. While Don and I travelled comfortably around the country having a laugh in the front of the van, our helpers had to stay in the back with the dogs and endure lengthy journeys, such as trips down to Dingle and home again on the same day. They had no seating, and had to put up with being thrown from side to side on bumpy, winding roads, most of which were dotted with potholes. Much of the time, they were exposed to harsh weather conditions, and their clothing back then was totally inadequate for protecting them from the cold and rain, as we didn't have the proper outdoor gear.

Hiding out could last six hours, and I often found my wife crying with the cold while hiding under a rock up a mountain, having waited for hours to be located by the dog. Once, while she was acting as a body and waiting to be found in a cave in Carrauntoohil, two children out for a walk with their parents happened to look in. Marie was sitting at the back of the cave, and when she saw them, she just said, 'Hi!' They got the shock of their lives, and ran off screaming. They probably thought they had found the 'mad woman' of the mountains. Marie ended up screaming herself, on another training session, when a herd of goats descended upon her when she was halfway up the Devil's Ladder. But she quickly hunted them by battering them with a fistful of stones.

As well as roping in the adults, my children Shane, Michelle and Gemma were also called upon to act as bodies, especially when I trained near home. Most evenings, one of them would willingly hide in a nearby field and wait to be found. These short, simple, fun sessions lasted only fifteen to twenty minutes. The purpose of this type of consistent training was to condition the dogs into believing that locating the missing person was their only mission in life. After supper, I usually hopped on my bicycle and took the dogs for a four-to-six-mile run on the roads around Knockraha, or I left the bicycle behind and jogged along with the dogs. On return from these exercise sessions, I then cycled or drove to the local woods in Ballyrea or Moanbaun. Don would arrive with his 'search' dog Rizzo, and we'd train from around 9 p.m. to midnight, often later.

Some evenings after work, I drove to The Vee in Lismore, usually with Don – or whoever I could persuade to come along – to train the dogs for a few hours. Other times, we headed for Gougane Barra, Glengarriff or the Hag's Glen. Under the instruction of Tom O'Neill from Midleton, I mastered the skills of reading a map and compass. Tom was well known for teaching navigation and survival skills to the Reserve Defence Forces. Very quickly, I realised that while learning the skills of map and compass reading was one thing, finding the time to practise them was quite another. I studied first-aid from beginner to mountain-rescue level. Once I acquired the knowledge, I practised it over and over again. Then I tackled abseiling and climbing techniques. I familiarised myself with ropes, harnesses, figures of eight and karabiners, which are large, steel spring clips used for hooking a person to another attachment for safety purposes.

As soon as I had gathered a collection of climbing gear, I began to carry it everywhere. I was constantly on the lookout for areas to practise abseiling. Whenever I saw a suitable spot, even at the side of the road, I set up a rope. Mike O'Shea from the Kerry Mountain Rescue Team often travelled up from Killarney and spent endless hours abseiling with Don and myself off the viaduct on the Cork to Bandon road. Now and again, I slotted an indoor climb into the week's training programme by practising at a climbing wall in Dromcollogher in north Cork.

At one point, I became obsessed with running as part of the training routine. When George Mallory, the famous mountaineer, was asked why he wanted to climb Mount Everest, he replied, 'Because it is there.' I know exactly what he meant. It's easy to become obsessed, with anything. When you get to a point where you realise you are good at something, that's when the adrenaline rush kicks in and you just don't want to give up. You're hooked. It's like driving down a one-way street – there's no turning back. Most days, at lunch time, I went for a sixty-minute run. Other days, I spent my lunch hour in the local gym. I never had the time for lunch, but, somehow, I never seemed to feel hungry. I lost a lot of weight during this period. On the way home, I'd run another four miles, starting from the Silver Springs Hotel. Sometimes, in the evenings, my son Shane would cycle alongside me as I jogged so as to help me increase my speed. I was always pushing myself, trying to go that extra mile. The better I became, the more I wanted to do. Then I started taking part in road races, from five miles up to half-marathons. I was happy if I finished in the top twenty per cent of any race. But then it all came to a sudden halt when I injured my ankle. That put an end to the running part of the training.

Most hillwalking clubs don't allow dogs on regular walks. When it came to choosing a hillwalking club to join, Don and I opted for the Killarney Mountaineering Club (KMC) because we knew our dogs would be welcomed there with open arms. The KMC began in 1981, and many of its walks took place around the local Macgillycuddy Reeks, the highest mountain range in Ireland. Our first walk with the KMC was one of the worst days of my life. Before setting out for Killarney, I visited my local army-surplus store and stocked up on some gear I thought would be ideal for hillwalking, including a framed backpack. I stuffed the backpack with mini Mars bars, a flask of soup, sandwiches, minerals, dog food, an aluminium dog bowl and, believe it or not, a two-litre container of water for the dog. I packed a compass and map, neither of which I could read at the time as I hadn't yet taken instruction on these skills from Tom O'Neill, but I thought that having them would greatly impress the other walkers in the group! I brought along my first search dog, a German shepherd named Dex. He came from a show line and was a grandson of double world *sieger*, or world champion, Uran Vom Wildsteiger Land and a son of German import Aro Vom Wiesenborn, son of Sieger Uran. Dex was an excellent show dog and had many show-ring wins to his credit. From the start, I was committed to using dogs with a show-line background. I wanted to prove that they were equally as good as working dogs, which are normally smaller, leaner and fitter. Accompanying Don was Rizzo, another descendant from a first-rate show line, and himself a brilliant show dog well advanced in *schutzhund* training. He was a son of a German import, the champion Alf Vom Quengelbach.

When we arrived in Killarney, members of the club – all strangers to us – began piling into our van. We quickly learned that using as few vehicles as possible was the norm as this saved parking space later at the starting point for the walk. Once everyone had squeezed themselves into some vehicle or other, we set off in convoy, following the lead car, which was barely hitting the road. Boy, was I scared! Jesus, I thought to myself, these people are going to kill me even before I set foot on a mountain. We raced on. Although they were all experienced hillwalkers and mountaineers, they acted like a pack of excited children, unable to contain their enthusiasm to begin the mountain climb.

At the starting point, everyone hopped out and chattered noisily as they sorted out their gear. Don and I looked on open-mouthed, like two little boys on their first day at school. They checked their backpacks for food, water, map, compass and rain gear. Apparently, Gore-tex jackets were the order of the day. Then they laced their boots firmly, put on gaiters, and secured their gloves and headgear in the backpack. And then it came to us. Here we were, the search-dog handlers from Cork with our very inadequate gear and, as was quickly spotted, a very dangerous design of backpack. Donie Sullivan – a member of both the KMC and the Kerry Mountain Rescue Team – took me aside and said that if the frame of my rucksack got caught on an outcrop of rock along a narrow ledge, it could knock me off the mountain as the frame protruded above my head. Even though I didn't leave it behind, as it was the only one I had, I learned from my mistake.

With all the checking of gear complete, we set off on our first hillwalk. Don was much younger than me, still only a teenager, and extremely fit. Foolishly, I believed I was equally as fit and would have no difficulty whatsoever with the walk. Earlier that week, I had read a book on hillwalking that advised that it was better to eat little but often when on a hillwalk. Taking this recommendation to the extreme, I began eating and drinking from the time I started the walk. All of a sudden, the pace became much faster than I'd expected. Climbing through heather and bogland was tough. I began to feel severe pain in my calves and thighs. After only an hour, I was sweating profusely. My head ached, my stomach churned. Eventually, I had to tell Don because I was convinced I was going to die! Don laughed and encouraged me to keep going or our so-called search-dog careers would be over before they'd begun. I looked around me. The group consisted of people of all ages; a woman in her sixties was sauntering along as though out for a Sunday stroll in the park.

Two hours later, struggling up steep ground, knee-deep in heather, I noticed Don had begun to lag behind. I waited for him to catch up. His knee was giving trouble and he couldn't walk any further. Some of the walkers who were also members of the rescue team came back to us. They manipulated and bandaged Don's knee. After a short rest, he was fine again and fit to continue.

During the walk different members walked alongside us and explained about hillwalking. At every rest point, they took out a map and showed us exactly where we were in relation to the starting point. Everybody was helpful, encouraging, non-judgemental and more than willing to teach us everything they knew about hillwalking.

Since we began the walk, the day had been wet and damp, with little streams of water flowing everywhere. Even so – and to everyone's amusement – I regularly took out Dex's bowl and poured some water from my container. After I had filled his bowl a few times, one of the group was brave enough to tell me there was no need to carry a container of water around as there was water everywhere.

That first, memorable, torturous hillwalk lasted six hours. Afterwards, as was customary, we all went to a local pub to have a mineral or two before setting out on the journey home. Some of the group joked that Don and I were a lazy pair as our dogs had pulled us up the hill. We'd kept the dogs on the leads all the way because we were afraid they'd chase sheep. We couldn't deny it, they'd helped us along. While the banter continued, I purchased minerals one after the other as my body was craving liquid. Later, my head began to throb and I started to throw up. On the two-hour journey home, we had to stop every few minutes as I was still getting sick. I felt under big pressure as I had to be back by 9 p.m. to do a gig. When we finally made it home, I jumped straight into my car and headed to work; time for a shower and a shave was out of the question. And I certainly didn't want any food.

Surprisingly, the following day I didn't have a pain or an ache. I felt totally rejuvenated and on a high. Instead of being depressed about my obvious lack of fitness and knowledge of hillwalking, I felt more determined than ever to become fit and to learn everything there was to know about hillwalking and mountaineering. From then on, Don and I became dedicated members of the KMC, and walked with the club every second Sunday.

On one such Sunday, the rain came teeming down as we arrived to climb Carrauntoohil. Having gone to the usual meeting place, we soon realised that the cute Kerry people had stayed in bed because of the bad weather, while us twits from Cork had turned up expecting the usual crowd. We waited to see if anyone else would come along. A woman arrived, all kitted out in new gear for the mountain. She asked if we were going climbing, told us she was a schoolteacher, and said this would be her very first climb. Her pupils were all looking forward to hearing about her day on Carrauntoohil, and she didn't want to go home without taking part in the climb. We told her that as we had driven all the way down to Killarney, we were going to go for a 'bit of a doddle' up the Hag's Glen and that she was more than welcome to join us. She accepted, and off we went. The Hag's Glen was flooded, with water pouring off the mountainside. After about an hour, the woman started to complain about her legs. I suggested we turn back, but she was having none of it, and was determined to continue regardless of cost or conditions. At the top of the Devil's Ladder, I tried once again to persuade her to call a halt, but she refused and we soldiered on. By now, she was limping badly and almost crying with pain. Every few hundred yards, she was stopping to sit down and rest. But she was insistent on carrying on with or without us. Going it alone was ridiculous, especially as visibility was down to a few yards, she didn't know the route to the top, and she had no map or compass. Even if she had, she probably wouldn't have been able to read them. Eventually, we made it to the cross at the top of Carrauntoohil. Having achieved her goal, she collapsed on the spot and told us she couldn't walk another step. After an hour of coaxing her, we finally managed to get her standing. We had to physically carry her down the mountain and back to the car park. Normally, this climb and descent would have taken us about five hours to complete; that day, it took nine hours. Doddle, how are you?

One of the more serious aspects of training with the KMC was to stock-proof our dogs, which meant teaching them to ignore farm livestock. We achieved this with the help of Joe Cronin, whose farmyard lies in the shadow of Carrauntoohil and at the start of the Hag's Glen. Before we'd set off on a climb, Joe would pen some of his sheep into a small paddock near his house, where we would practise some obedience and control work with our dogs around the sheep. This was very helpful as it was vital that our dogs did not chase sheep on the hill.

All of the Cronin family were good friends to search-and-rescue people. They allowed us to use their yard for parking and as a base for rescues on Carrauntoohil. After a climb, Mrs Cronin always had tea and sandwiches ready for us. She looked after non-members, too, and quickly notified the rescue team if any walkers failed to return to the yard by nightfall to collect their cars. Her son Gerard regularly acted as a body for us on the mountain. John, another son, owned an excellent golden retriever called Sandy, a dog well on the way to becoming a search-and-rescue dog. Even our dogs appeared to recognise the kindness of the Cronins, as I discovered after one particular training session on Carrauntoohil. On that day, dog handlers, including Neil, had travelled from all over Ireland to take part in the training. We based ourselves in Cronins' yard, and returned there after the session for a debriefing. As normal, our dogs ran loose around the yard. As I packed up our gear to set off for home, I couldn't find any trace of Dex. When Mrs Cronin heard me calling his name, she appeared at the door with a big smile on her face and beckoned me to come inside. There was Dex lying in front of a roaring fire having scavenged everything he could off the table.

While walking with the KMC, our dogs were regularly fed sandwiches by all and sundry. As a result, whenever we came across walkers eating, we shouted at them, 'Mind your sandwiches!' On one particular walk known as the Reeks Walk, the dogs made sure to get their fill. The Reeks Walk is a traditional, annual, nine-hour walk around the Macgillycuddy Reeks, in which people from all over the country take part. Usually, the Kerry Mountain Rescue Team, together with other volunteers, staff way stations along the route to provide rescue cover for any walkers who might get into difficulty. On our first year of hillwalking, Don and I decided to join in this long-established walk. As we arrived late, we agreed to link up with the walk on the Devil's Ladder. The mountain was covered in fog and mist, visibility was very poor, and the dogs began ranging ahead of us. Within minutes, they had disappeared up the Devil's Ladder and high into the mist. As they were both stock-proofed and knew the area well, we took little notice. It didn't bother us at all that they were no longer in view. About ten minutes later, we heard screams and then peals of laughter coming out of the mist. The dogs ran back down to us and indicated a find by barking. We climbed until we finally reached the top of the Ladder – a small plateau of grass and mud around ten foot square – only to find ourselves in the centre of about fifteen women. The women explained that they were participants in the Reeks Walk and had decided to stop for a rest and some food. Laughing, they recalled their terror at seeing the two 'wolves' emerge from the mist, and running wildly from person to person and grabbing all their sandwiches. Luckily, their fears quickly vanished as one of the group was a regular climber of Carrauntoohil and recognised the dogs.

Training with the Kerry Mountain Rescue Team was both a challenge and an honour, especially for us amateurs. (The team was formed in 1966 following the death of two mountain climbers in the south-west. Since then, it has been on constant call-out to rescue climbers and walkers in distress.) With the Kerry Mountain Rescue Team, we were trained in and tested on all aspects of mountain rescue, including stretcher carrying over rough ground, stretcher lowering off cliffs, abseiling, mountain-rescue first aid, night navigation, and jumaring (rope climbing). We practised being lowered off and raised onto the mountain with the dogs secured to us with special harnesses. Medics, stretcher bearers and the Air Corps trained with us. Realistic scenarios were set up. Once the live body was located, the rest of the team swung swiftly into action.

After several months of training, the Kerry Mountain Rescue Team began to call Don and me to real-life searches. Even though our dogs were not yet certified search dogs, the team leader gave permission for the dogs to accompany us on searches. This gave us valuable experience. From then on, getting a phone call at 2 a.m. became very exciting as it signalled a call-out, or 'shout' as it's known. Once the shout came, I'd jump out of bed, grab my gear, get my dog and meet Don somewhere convenient, from where we'd drive to the rescue base. Many times, false alarms occurred, and call-outs were subsequently cancelled. But that was well before the arrival of mobile phones, which meant that if we had already set out we had to travel all the way to the rescue base before learning of the cancellation. Often, I returned home after a false alarm and headed straight for work with little or no sleep.

We took part in the search for an English climber whose car had been found abandoned in a car park near the Hag's Glen after he failed to return from a climb on the Macgillycuddy Reeks. Having completed an investigation, the gardaí decided to conduct a search. As Dex and Rizzo were not certified, search teams from Northern Ireland, England and Wales were called, and, being members of the local rescue team, Don and I were asked to act as guides for these handlers. The handler I was guiding around the mountain was older than me but, boy, was he fit. Just walking and talking to him throughout the search made me realise that these men and women were on a very different level to us. At first, it may not have been noticeable, but it soon became clear that their hill fitness and dog-handling skills were outstanding. I learned so much during that particular search simply by talking to them and observing their actions. Unfortunately, the search teams failed to find the missing man, and eventually the search was called off.

Six months later, Don and I were in final preparations before heading to Cumbria in England to have our dogs assessed as mission-ready search dogs. We had arranged to train in the Hag's Glen with members of the Killarney Mountain Rescue Team and some volunteers from our families. At this stage, after almost two years of continual training, search dogs should be capable of ranging up to a half-mile from their handlers. They should be trusted to continue searching on their own and to return occasionally to within earshot or sight of the handlers. To determine if a dog has reached this level of training, engaging an observer who will use both binoculars and a two-way radio is essential. While the dog and handler work on one side of a valley, the observer stays on the opposite hill and watches the dog closely, especially when the dog is out of sight of the handler. The observer keeps the handler informed on what the dog is doing. For example, is the dog chasing sheep? Is the dog continuing to work? Everything must be reported as it happens. If the dog continues to work when out of sight, the handler can develop confidence in the dog. This is important, as one of the biggest problems in search-dog training is handler confidence. The handlers must always ask, Do I trust the dogs to do the job for which they have been trained?

On that particular training day, Don was searching underneath Carrauntoohil on very dangerous ground. A number of bodies were in position around the cliff's face, including Don's brother Tom, who was close to the bottom of the hill. I was acting as an observer, and positioned myself on the hill opposite. An hour or so into the search, Tom made radio contact. He had found a backpack under a ledge near his hiding place. I told him to leave it for a while. Soon after, he contacted me again to say he had noticed a watch in a stream just beneath him; it was still functioning and showing the right time. He thought the backpack and watch might have been lying there for some time. Straight away, I contacted Con Moriarty, leader of the Kerry Mountain Rescue Team. Con was acting as one of the bodies for the day. He suggested we carry on and complete our training session first.

After several hours, we finished our training. Everyone gathered where Tom had found the backpack and watch. The group included the renowned Pat Falvey, a fellow club member. From where we stood, the cliff face above was to the right of the Devil's Ladder and, in places, rising vertically to the summit of Carrauntoohil. Con and Pat climbed directly up from where the backpack was lying. After only a few hundred feet, they came upon a body. Con made contact on the radio to tell us, and several of us climbed up to the location, where we saw the intact skeleton of a person. A camera and a pair of binoculars hung around the neck of the skeleton. His hat was still on his head and his feet were covered with his shoes. Con contacted the gardaí, and between them they concluded that these were the remains of the missing Englishman whom we had failed to locate six months previously. After Con had taken some photographs for the coroner, we all said some prayers before placing the remains in a bivvy bag. As the area was hazardous, we had to rope the remains down the cliff and take turns in carrying the deceased out of the Hag's Glen. We walked in silence back to our vehicles at Lisleibane, where a hearse with a coffin met us. While everyone was very sad at finding the body, we felt that it might, at least, offer a degree of closure to his family.

As I had never before seen the remains of a human on a hill, the experience was a revelation to me. It made me realise the importance of what we were doing. With or without dogs, search-and-rescue work is not a game. People's lives and their families can be affected by our actions. I reminded myself that this could have been someone I knew or even a family member. From that moment on, I became more determined than ever to succeed in getting my dog certified.

In the early days of training with Neil, I had become his worst nightmare, mainly because of my previous experience of training dogs for obedience, or *schutzhund*. While I'd listen attentively to Neil's advice at training sessions in the Wicklow Mountains or Mourne Mountains, later, at home,

I'd decide that I knew better, and would revert to my old methods of training. As a result, it took me much longer than necessary to train my first search dog. I have since become convinced that the person who learns quickest is the person who has absolutely no knowledge of dog training, provided, of course, that the commitment to learn is strong. The saying that 'a little knowledge is a dangerous thing' is very true. First and foremost, I was a dog handler, and I viewed search-dog training as just another aspect of my career in dogs. In Britain, the opposite was true of those involved in search and rescue. Above all else, British search-dog handlers were mountaineers, and they took up search-dog handling as another aid to rescue training. As they were very experienced in mountaineering, navigation and first aid, they were extremely valuable as members of their local rescue teams. I was doing things the opposite way around.

Every sixth Friday, Don and I left Cork at 6 p.m. with the dogs to begin a three-hour drive to Laragh, County Wicklow, for SARDA training weekends with Neil. Most of the other dog handlers would have arrived before us, along with some members of the local mountain-rescue teams, who would have offered to act as bodies for the weekend. Having settled ourselves into the hut, which was a hostel run by the Dublin and Wicklow mountain-rescue teams, we'd start up a sing-song, with both Neil and myself on guitar. Neil had a huge collection of funny songs, with songs sung by Burl Ives among his favourites. All our dogs were outside in their owners' vans, which would be their sleeping quarters for the weekend.

In the morning, Neil was always first to rise. Having tended to his dog, he'd put on a big fry-up of rashers and sausages. After breakfast, in his role as training officer, he'd take his first group of bodies to the hill and place them in position for the more advanced dogs. The rest of us would follow an hour later. Regardless of weather, training always went ahead. Fair-weather sailors were not welcome on dog-training weekends. In advance, training areas would have been set up by Neil to correspond with the number of dog teams taking part and the number of bodies available. Areas varied in size, from fifteen-minute areas to three-hour areas. Each area lay within certain boundaries, such as skyline, gullies and pathways. Once the handler understood the area and informed Neil on how it was proposed to cover it, the simulated search got underway.

For the hill search, handlers had to be fully clothed in orange, red or yellow, as these bright colours stand out from the surroundings. They had to carry full backpacks, as they would on a real search. This meant that they had to bring a Carry Mat (a foam mattress), warm gear, rain gear, spare gear, a map, compass, head torch, spare batteries, whistle, food and liquids for two days, and a bivvy bag (an orange, plastic survival bag, similar to a mini tent and six feet in length). Often, people packed two bivvy bags as they could be laid in the form of a cross to attract attention. Dry clothes at base were also essential.

Throughout the search, the training officer and handler kept in constant communication through two-way radios. Neil never lost his cool with any of the handlers, and always remained extremely calm. On completion of the search, the handler returned to base, where a debriefing took place. The handler explained in detail how the search was conducted and why certain actions were carried out while on the hill, allowing for the lay of the land, wind direction and the dog's attitude. Generally, depending on the handler's account, Neil would then make a few suggestions as to how the search might have been conducted more efficiently.

After a short rest, the handler and dog were given a second area to search, and were expected to implement Neil's recommendations. Usually, two or three dog teams worked different areas at the same time. This made Neil's job very difficult as he had to try to watch each team as it worked through an area while writing notes for each debriefing. While the area searches were in progress, other potential handlers observed in the hope of improving their own knowledge and skills of search-dog handling. During the two days, if there was time, these beginners were usually given some training with the more experienced handlers.

As is traditional in search-dog training, walk-out time was 3 p.m. This meant that the bodies left their hiding places and returned to base regardless of whether or not they were found. At this point, a further and more detailed debriefing took place back at the hostel. This session included not only Neil and the handlers but also the bodies, who had to describe how each dog reacted on the find, or if they came close to finding the body. They also had to give an account of the subsequent interaction between the dog and handler on completion of the search sequence. Handlers took notes as they needed to show improvement the following day. A training log was kept by each handler, which was signed by the training officer after each training weekend.

Sunday's session was important as it was used mainly to correct any niggling training problems that might have surfaced on the Saturday. Training finished at 3 p.m., when Don and I would head back to Cork, usually getting home around 8 p.m. On Monday nights, still feeling invigorated after the weekend, I was eager to begin again the home routine of training and to rectify any errors made in Wicklow.

November 1989 came round. Don and I had a pre-assessment in the Wicklow Hills under a very experienced search-dog assessor from the Lakes Mountain Rescue Team in Cumbria. In previous years, we had both attended an English mountain-rescue-dog assessment as observers. We knew well what to expect. Unfortunately, the pre-assessment went badly. Doubt was cast on my own and on Dex's ability to pass a search-dog assessment. Thankfully – after some discussion and argument – Neil, who as training officer had complete control, decided to let me go. As the assessment was still a few months away, I felt confident that I had enough time to correct my mistakes. For Don and me, this was our final run-in. During the following months, we trained and exercised non-stop with the dogs to the exclusion of all else. At this stage, Dex was almost four years old and Rizzo was five. We estimated that we had spent at least fifteen hundred hours training and that the training of each dog had cost £20,000.

As we were the first handlers and dogs from the Republic

of Ireland to apply for qualification, we received much publicity from the local media. Because of the media hype, I was fortunate enough to receive a very generous donation of £400. However, when I brought the cheque to work with the intention of cashing it, midway through the morning I discovered it was missing. Minutes later, a clerk at my local bank in the South Mall phoned. She said a man claiming to be me was standing at her counter and trying to cash my cheque. When she had asked him why the cheque had been issued to him, he gave her the full background to the forthcoming trip for assessment, which of course was common knowledge because of the media coverage. By now, she had phoned the gardaí and the man was still waiting for the cash. I rushed off to the bank. A garda had just arrived before me. He tapped the man on the shoulder and asked, 'Are you Mick McCarthy?' When the man replied that he was, the garda said, 'Well, that's funny, because the real Mick McCarthy is standing right behind you.' It transpired that a customer at my place of work had stolen the cheque, and that the man at the bank had bought it from the thief for £40.

In April 1990, after all the hype and drama, Don, Dex, Rizzo and I were ready to set off for Ennerdale in Cumbria for our first official assessment. Tim Murphy accompanied us from Kerry, together with Don's brother Tom, both of whom had been roped in to act as bodies. Regardless of all the good wishes we received, Don and I were very aware that some among the doggy community here doubted our ability to succeed. They had made it quite clear that they thought we were doomed to failure and that our aspirations were unrealistic. We were also conscious of the fact that German shepherds were not at all popular in England as search-and-rescue dogs. Only one thing was certain – we had a lot to prove.

Cumbria

After a seven-hour drive from Holyhead, we finally arrived at Ennerdale in Cumbria and made our way to High Gillerthwaite Farm, which was situated several miles in along a forest track. We were met by two of the assessors who would carry out the assessments on the nearby mountains. When we opened the door of the dog trailer, one of the assessors immediately said, 'Oh, bloody mutton eaters!' The other made a comment about the fun they usually have when 'Alsatians' get in amongst the sheep. At this stage, my blood was boiling. I was on the verge of closing up the dog trailer, turning round and heading straight back home, but I did not. They continued to try to get the wind up us by saying that there was only one German shepherd working in England as a mountain-rescue dog, mainly because handlers had found it extremely difficult to livestock-proof a German shepherd. In our experience, Don and I had found otherwise. We never had any difficulty in teaching our dogs to ignore farm livestock. In our initial training, the only problems we had were not with our dogs at all but with our own lack of knowledge and experience in training dogs for the intricacies of searching. Of course, as I have already mentioned, mountain-rescue-dog handlers in other countries are primarily mountaineers, not doggy people. As members of mountain-rescue teams, they take up dog handling as a means to an end: namely, the quick and efficient searching of a mountain to locate a missing person. Generally, when choosing a puppy to train as a search dog, foreign handlers look for a breed that is socially acceptable to farmers and the public, one easy to train and which does not carry the 'bad dog' tag of 'Alsatian'. All the negative talk about German shepherds got Don and me off to a bad start, but it also made us more determined than ever to prove that our dogs were not sheep chasers.

During the night, thanks to the constant snoring of one of my travelling companions – who shall remain nameless – I got little sleep. The following morning, I woke with a splitting headache, rose at 6 a.m. to have breakfast, and went for a walk with the dogs in the hope that the country air might clear my head. At 7 a.m., when I came back to the farmyard, I found that some of the assessors had already left for the mountains with their bodies. Among those bodies were our own helpers, Tim and Tom.

Detective Sergeant Dave Riley arrived to give the briefing on what was expected of us during the first days of searches. At 8 a.m. Don and I set out for a ninety-minute guided walk up very steep, wooded mountainside to our search areas. Each of us was given a search area on opposite sides of a valley. I was the first lamb to the slaughter, and my area – Area 1 – was carefully pointed out to me. It looked huge. Starting on the right-hand boundary, it continued up a snow-covered gully to a col, which from where I stood appeared to be miles away in the distance. At an angle from the col, the top boundary led to the left, down underneath almost vertical crags. Then, after about five hundred yards, it went back up to the skyline and along the top for about half a mile. The remnants of a stone wall formed the left-hand boundary, which led from the valley floor right up almost to the skyline, and was only visible from base by using binoculars. A stream marked the bottom boundary, flowing just underneath us at base and going right down the valley floor. On the opposite side, Don's area looked equally large and even more treacherous. Being located on the shaded side of the valley, it contained much more snow and ice.

My instructions were to search the area within the boundaries given and to report by radio anything I found within those limits. During the annual SARDA England mountain-rescue-dog assessment – held every February – the large number of dogs being judged meant the areas allocated were usually much smaller than those Don and I were given. However, as we'd been warned, there were only two of us for assessment and we were going to be 'put through the grinder'. As with *schutzhund* trials, I had to present myself to the assessors to explain to them how I intended to search my area and how my dog would indicate a find. To check if a body had been placed at the start, I began my search by walking twenty to thirty feet to the right of my right-hand boundary. Within a few minutes of sending Dex up the hill, he disappeared out of sight. Later, I spotted him ranging up along the right-hand boundary, several hundred yards in front of me. Soon, I was trudging through snow. Although this slowed me up a lot, it seemed to make no difference to Dex. Having walked for twenty minutes, I had only covered less than half of my right-hand boundary. At this stage, I could hear Rizzo barking across the valley, and I became a little disheartened as I knew he had made a find.

Still moving towards the col, Dex had almost reached the top. As he had already covered that area, this meant I didn't have to walk that far. Putting my head down, I decided to plough on for a bit longer. Within minutes, I heard a bark. It took me a while before I eventually made out the faint shape of Dex high up on the crags to my left. As he was well above the boundary, I began to worry. I prayed silently that it wasn't a false alarm. Then the words of Neil Powell came ringing in my ears: 'Always trust your dog' – words that returned to haunt me in later years when I was involved in a search for an eleven-year-old boy in Midleton. My heart pounded with excitement as Dex continued to bark. I began climbing to my left towards the crags. Sure enough, Dex came running down towards me, still barking. This was his way of indicating, of telling me that this was the area to search. When I said the magic words, 'Show me', he immediately turned and headed back up the crags. Every so often, he stopped, turned and barked back at me. By then, I was positive he had made a find. I climbed up the crags and continued over ice-encrusted snow for about fifteen minutes. At last, I spotted the body hidden in a hole in the rocks. I was relieved and delighted to find the body. But I was also annoyed as the body was not within the boundaries pointed out to me at the start. If I had seen the dog straying outside the boundaries, I would have called him back as I would have considered it a waste of time and energy searching outside the designated area.

In the meantime, back at base, the assessors were anxiously awaiting my radio report. By using their binoculars, they had seen Dex climb up into the crags and beyond the boundary. They were extremely annoyed that the body had moved from its original location without telling them, and were very generous in praising Dex for making such a good find.

Using Dex to search between me and the skyline, I continued the search back underneath the top boundary until I arrived at the wall representing the left-hand margin. As the area was very large, I decided to search it in three or four sweeps. I dropped down to the left-hand boundary. With the wind to my back, I began searching the central section of my area. Across, in front, Dex was working in a zigzag fashion, ranging out about three hundred yards either side of me. Just as I had almost finished the middle section, Dex struck again. This time, the body was down underneath, towards the bottom boundary and a little behind us. As the wind was coming from behind, Dex did not strike until he had moved ahead of the area containing the body. I could see him running down into a section of rocks and boulders. Having run around the rocks for some time, he began barking. Straight away, I knew that the body was in an inaccessible spot. Dex ran back towards me still barking. His indication was excellent. When I gave the command, 'Show me', he again took me back to the rocks, and continued to search for a way through to the body. Having climbed over the rocks, I finally found the body at the bottom of a hole, ten feet deep. To allow Dex to see the source of fun and games, I brought the body out with me. Whether just practising or conducting real-life searches, the dog should always regard the search as great fun. Having told base that we had located a second body, Dex and I took a fifteen-minute rest before continuing and finishing the area.

Back at base, the assessors questioned me on how I thought the search had gone. Before answering, I thought carefully as I felt my reply could be the deciding factor in persuading the assessors that I was capable of handling a search dog efficiently. Did I trust my dog enough? Was I convinced that there were no more bodies in the area? Did I use the dog efficiently? Fortunately, the assessors seemed satisfied with my replies, and I was asked to wait until Don had completed his area. When Don returned, the assessors began to put him through his debriefing. Don and I were forbidden to speak to each other so as to ensure we didn't give away any secrets about our individual areas.

During lunch break, one of the assessors contacted the bodies by radio and asked them to relocate. Once everyone was in position, we were ready to begin again. Don was sent off to search Area 1. About ten minutes later, I was sent out to clear Area 2, which consisted almost completely of steep crags with many scree slopes leading up into gullies. Generally, gullies can be difficult to search, and often it becomes necessary for the handlers themselves to actually physically search a gully. The search went well. By 6.30 p.m., Don and I had both completed our second areas and located all bodies.

Every evening, the seven assessors held a meeting, which usually lasted several hours. They discussed the merits or demerits of each handler and dog team. All seven assessors were asked if they would be happy to take a particular team on a search. If any one of the assessors expressed a doubt, that team was deemed to have failed. After the assessors' first meeting, Don and I were told that we had both been given a borderline pass. They explained that the borderline pass was given because they felt that we had cheated: supposedly I had informed Don where the bodies in the first area were located, which would have been very near the spot to which the bodies were moved for Don's assessment. The assessors found it difficult to believe that our dogs could be as competent as they appeared.

On the second morning, searches took place in a new area on very steep ground. Much of the area was covered in knee-deep heather, with a few boulder fields thrown in for good measure. On steep ground in particular, heather is very tiring and difficult to walk through, both for the dog and the handler. However, this is where the power of the German shepherd comes to the fore. A fit German shepherd can force his way up through this type of heavy terrain. In contrast, smaller dogs, such as the collie, can find the going very difficult.

In the afternoon, the search took place on a very large tract of open, hilly ground on which several sheep were grazing peacefully. Being aware that the assessors had a preconceived notion that a German shepherd was bound to make an attempt at chasing the sheep, we were intent on showing them that the dogs were well stock-proofed. From the beginning, Dex ranged out a few hundred yards ahead of me. Immediately, he found himself in amongst sheep. When they saw him, they scattered to the four winds. But Dex stuck to his task. He ignored the sheep, as did Rizzo when it was his turn to search the area. In less than ninety minutes, both dogs had cleared their areas and located all bodies.

Later that evening, Don and I were taken aback to learn that we would have to conduct a third search, which was to take place in a large forest. As we entered the forest, Dex and Rizzo were in their element. As most of their midweek training at home had taken place on this type of ground, they felt totally at home. Both dogs completed a find in a very short time. Our second day drew to a close, and after the assessors' meeting, we learned that we had both passed the day's tests.

The following morning, having driven a further three miles in along the forest path, we came to a clearing that contained a rescue hut. We had to wait there for about an hour while the assessors positioned the bodies for our next test. As this was the last day of our assessment, some other assessors had come along to observe. Don was called in first, started his area and quickly disappeared out of sight. As I walked towards the base, the forest gave way to a beautiful, clean valley, surrounded on each side with very high, rolling ground, topped again with snow-covered crags. After about twenty minutes, I reached base and was shown my area. As it was very popular with walkers and climbers, many difficulties could arise when searching with a dog for a missing person. On that day, the local mountain-rescue team was conducting a training session in the area, and this could cause further confusion for the dog as the area would be criss-crossed with fresh scents. The assessors accepted that we would have a hard time, but we knew they wanted to find out how the dogs would cope with so many different scents, and how we would handle them under such circumstances.

After presenting myself to the assessors, I set off with Dex. Having checked the direction of the wind, I decided to work from right to left along the top half of my area. As this was going to be the toughest part, I opted to start at the top while Dex was relatively fresh. The search went off without a hitch. We cleared the area in less than three hours, and found all bodies. As Don's area was much larger than mine, it took a little longer to finish.

Once Don had completed his area, the assessors held a short meeting. Afterwards, they told us they had seen enough and there would be no need for us to conduct a second search that day. We were both officially informed that we had passed our search-dog assessment. Passing the Novice Search Dog test meant that Don and I were now mission-ready search-dog handlers, and could go on call-outs. The assessors apologised for having ever doubted our dogs or us. The chief coordinator of SARDA England congratulated us on the exceptionally high standard of work maintained by Don, myself and the dogs over the three-day period. He acknowledged that the performance of our dogs had succeeded in changing the assessors' and observers' opinions of German shepherds, and said that he hoped to see more German shepherds qualifying as search-and-rescue dogs in the near future.

It took several days after arriving home for our feet to touch the ground. Rizzo and Dex were now the first and only qualified search-and-rescue dogs in the Republic of Ireland. It had taken nearly four years of very hard work for Don, myself, our dogs, our families, friends and other helpers. But in the end it was worth it all. On hearing of our success, a delighted Con Moriarty – team leader of the Kerry Mountain Rescue Team – said, 'This is the biggest development for us since we opened a mountain rescue station in Killorglin in 1983. It's something we've been working towards for a long time.'

For our dogs to move from novice search dogs to full search grade, we had to pass a second assessment held later to confirm the initial grading and to ensure that handlers continued to retain high training standards after qualification. Unfortunately, Don and Rizzo were unable to go. Nevertheless, as Rizzo had passed the first assessment, his qualification still stood. At this second assessment, Dex was successful once again. Highly impressed with Dex's standard, the assessors expressed surprise that an 'Alsatian' would range as far as a collie.

Now Dex was the first and only full-graded international mountain-rescue search dog in the Republic of Ireland. Once again, Dex received much publicity and praise from the media here at home. However, we were not allowed to bask in the glory for very long. While the majority of the doggy people were thrilled with our success, some begrudgers among them viewed our accomplishment as a mere fluke. Given that full search dogs must undergo further assessments every three years so as to maintain the high standards of the initial two assessments, I decided that, instead of waiting, I would enter Dex for other assessments in the hope of silencing the begrudgers. In November 1990 Don and I went to Wales to take part in a SARDA Wales assessment. Again, this appraisal was held over three days in wet and wintry conditions. Once more, we achieved success.

In February 1991 I took Dex to Keswick in Cumbria to take part in assessments for upgrading. As it happened, Rizzo had a viral infection and was unable to take part, but Don was invited along as a trainee assessor. This major event was scheduled as a four-day assessment, beginning on Saturday 23 February. More than 150 mountain-rescue people from several countries were expected to attend, including commanding officers from army dog-training schools in both Norway and Sweden, together with their chief trainers. Having arrived on the Friday night, I fed and exercised Dex. Next morning, after an anxious, sleepless night, I rose at 6 a.m. When I checked on Dex, I found to my horror that he had devoured all his spare food – six days' ration. This was a bad start, and I became even more nervous.

Searching that day proved extremely difficult for both handler and dog because of gale-force winds and driving rain. In late afternoon, the winds eased and a dense mist moved in across the landscape. This reduced visibility to ten to fifteen feet. It was a very long, hard day, and I was more than relieved to be told I had passed, despite the bad weather and Dex's eating binge! All tests must be passed to qualify (though a repeat is allowed in certain circumstances, such as when an assessor has given incorrect information to a dog handler).

On Sunday and Monday the weather conditions improved a little, but the days were equally long and hard. Once again, we got through and without too much difficulty. On Sunday, in between searches, two English radio stations interviewed me, and I had the added pressure of being followed for two days by the Norwegian and Swedish delegations. As they worked mainly with German shepherd dogs themselves, they were especially interested in watching Dex work. On the Sunday night, a Swedish army colonel gave a lecture and video show. He commented on the very high standard of all the dogs in the assessment, particularly the German shepherd dog – the only German shepherd to take part in the assessment. He went on to say that their own German shepherds tended to tire and lose interest when they'd worked for six to eight hours, whereas Dex appeared to get fresher as the day went on.

Again, the fourth and final day of the assessment was very wet. At this stage, the assessors were checking the dogs for stamina, fitness and willingness to work, even when tired. Unbelievably, this was our best day as Dex worked almost without command, except for the occasional directional signal. Over the four days, Dex was one of only two dogs to find all of the bodies.

That night, certificates were presented during a dinner at the Keswick Hotel, where all the participants had stayed. I found it a very emotional occasion. As I walked back to my table having received my qualification certificate, I felt extremely proud of Dex, and I was convinced that this achievement would surely silence the begrudgers, if only for a while. Delighted with our achievements, Don and I believed that both Dex and Rizzo would play an important role in search-and-rescue operations for many years to come. We were wrong.

Castleisland Call-out

D on and I were raring to go, to get into the thick of it, anxious to do our bit for search and rescue. The first shout came when a farmer went missing on a mountain between Castleisland and Ballydesmond. We were called in with other members of SARDA – among them Neil Powell – two other searchers from Northern Ireland and one from Dublin. By then, the farmer had been missing for a number of days. The missing man lived on the opposite side of a mountain to his daughter, and climbed the mountain every Friday to visit her as part of his weekly routine. When he failed to turn up on one particular Friday during the summer, she sensed he was in trouble and reported him missing.

Local volunteers and Civil Defence members were searching on the mountain when we arrived on a fine, bright afternoon. As all of our SARDA dogs worked by air-scenting, we needed the mountain free from all human scent other than that of the missing man, and we asked the gardaí to clear the mountain of all other searchers and climbers before we could begin. Around 4 p.m. we started. We prepared to do a line search by spreading out about 400 yards apart. All of the dog handlers climbed up in a straight line and worked the dogs by sending them in a zigzag direction, over and back between opposite handlers. The mountain resembled a rounded hill. The climb was steep and the going was tough as the ground was boggy and covered in heather, with much forest growth in the valleys. We knew that the locals had carved out their own pathways up the mountain, but these were not obvious to us. More than likely, the farmer followed the exact same path every Friday, but we had no idea where it might be.

We continued to climb, though with no inkling of which direction the farmer might have taken. Every now and again, the handlers contacted each other on their walkie-talkies, especially when they felt it necessary to strengthen up on certain areas or ease off on others. Dex and I had almost reached the top of the mountain. By then, I was probably about a quarter of a mile from the nearest handler. On the mountain peak, Dex indicated. When I went to investigate, I found a man walking along the top. When I asked him what he was doing up there, he said he was looking for the missing farmer and knew him well. He also said he knew the area inside out as he often hunted there with the harriers. I pleaded with him to leave, and explained that we couldn't carry out a proper search if he stayed as the dogs would keep coming back to him, but he insisted on continuing to look for the missing man. I accept that he was a well-meaning member of the public, but because of his presence there was no point in our combing further through that particular area. I contacted Neil and told him I was coming down.

We searched until 8 p.m. before calling a halt, as the gardaí were expecting the arrival of 150 local volunteers to carry out a line search. Neil advised the gardaí that the locals should begin their search down at the point where we had finished. I suggested that they start high because the man would have been trying to go over the mountain. Just one hour later, the missing farmer was found on the top of the mountain, only a hundred yards from where Dex and I had stopped searching. He was lying on his back in an open plateau of ground with his hands crossed on his chest, laid out perfectly, almost as if he knew his end was near. As little dots of blood were found on his body, the detectives were called in to check him before the removal of his remains.

The volunteers came back down from the mountain, while a garda made his way up to stay with the body until the detectives arrived. The handlers climbed up to the scene with their dogs, with the Civil Defence following close behind with a stretcher. When we reached the top, the dogs indicated. But only the two German shepherds, Rizzo and Dex, dared go near the body. Dogs react differently to the scent of a dead body. Eiger, my retriever-collie-cross, was also with our group. When he entered the scent cone, he jumped back suddenly as if he had been hit by an electric fence.

We said a prayer over the deceased and remained with him, waiting for the arrival of the detectives. On examination of the body, they quickly ruled out foul play as they found that the spots of blood had been caused simply by exposure to the wilderness. The man had died of a heart attack.

Dex and Rizzo had taken part in their first search operation since qualifying in Cumbria.

Rizzo

In May 1991 a man was reported missing on Mount Brandon. Don and I got the shout. We quickly gathered our gear and headed to Kerry with the dogs. When we arrived, the search was already well underway, with members of the Kerry Mountain Rescue Team scattered on the mountain, combing their way through, as Air Corps helicopters circled overhead. The day was clear and visibility was excellent.

At the briefing, we learned that the missing man was an English tourist who was staying in a local guest house. The previous day, he had told the owner of the house that he was going off to climb Mount Brandon, and said he would return later to collect his belongings. When he failed to turn up, the landlady reported him missing.

Having decided on our starting points, we set off. Don and Rizzo climbed up towards the top of the mountain to begin a downward search, while Dex and I started upwards from the bottom. We combed Mount Brandon for several hours. Don, Rizzo and Con Moriarty were scouring the area along the top and down the sides of Faha Ridge when Rizzo began to search on some very steep ground. He came to a deep gully, leaped across it without hesitation or fear, and landed on the other side on a tiny ledge of jet-black rock. Because of the constant water fall, the rock was as smooth as ice. Rizzo slipped and fell awkwardly on his side. If he wanted to come back, he would have to turn around. But could he do it? It was almost impossible. He had no space to manoeuvre and the rock was too slippery, too treacherous. As he tried to get up, he found himself facing the gully. He was now in a very dangerous position, with no room to make even the slightest movement. He lost his footing and in the blink of an eye plunged down several hundred feet to his death.

Don contacted me on the radio. I listened in disbelief. My heart went out to Don: he had lost his best friend. We were all in shock, not only at the suddenness of Rizzo's death but also at our own vulnerability to the dangers lurking around us. The accident heightened our awareness of how the same fate could be met by any one of the human rescuers who place their lives on the line every time they take part in a search. But when dogs work ahead of their handlers they are always putting themselves at risk, testing the ground, protecting us humans from injury or fatality, minimising the dangers to searchers. At the end of the day, they're the guinea pigs. Apart from being a great working dog, Rizzo had been a brilliant show dog, with a beautiful temperament. Dex had lost a partner, too. All the endless days and nights of training flashed before me, as well as the trials and excitement of Cumbria. What had it all been for?

The helicopter crew had seen Rizzo fall. They winched a man down for his body, wrenched him up, airlifted him and took him back to Seán O'Dowd's pub in Cloghane, a pretty Gaeltacht village situated on the northern tip of the Dingle Peninsula and overlooking Brandon Bay.

Rizzo's death was a major setback. But there was no time for mourning – that would come later. A man was missing on the mountain. We immediately continued the search, deeply concerned for the safety of the tourist, fully intent on rescuing him. After two days of intensive searching, all our efforts proved fruitless. We never found the Englishman.

Seán O'Dowd – who had Cork connections and had taught for many years in the North Monastery before retiring from teaching – very kindly offered us a burial ground for Rizzo in the rear garden of his pub. Knowing how upset we were at Rizzo's death, Seán suggested Don and I should head back to Cork, and said he would bury him. We drove back in silence, still numbed that Rizzo was no longer with us, unable to voice our pain, our loss. Dex sat in the back of the van, alone, his partner and constant companion now gone forever.

Some time later, the missing tourist turned up at a guest house in Galway. It seems he had never set foot on Mount Brandon at all, but had invented the lie about going there to avoid paying for his stay. He had done a runner. Eventually, the scoundrel was arrested in England when he tried again to flee a guest house without paying the bill. All of us had paid a price in searching for him. As well as losing Rizzo, most of the searchers, including myself, had lost two days in wages. Knowing that Rizzo had died needlessly made his death even harder to accept.

Soon after the death of Rizzo, Don was invited to London by a major dog-food company to be presented with an award in recognition of the fact that Rizzo had died in the service of mankind. Don was lucky to have another dog in training at the time – Ben, a collie, drawing close to the qualification stage – and that helped keep him occupied, though it did not take away the pain of losing Rizzo.

The begrudgers – some members of the German Shepherd Association among them – were still implying that qualifying Dex and Rizzo had been a mere fluke. We heard the comments, and because of the serious nature of search-and-rescue work, we didn't want anyone doubting our dogs' abilities. We needed everyone, especially the gardaí, to have full confidence in the dogs, as in many search-and-rescue operations people's lives can be at stake. So to reassure everyone, we had already set out to qualify a second pair of dogs. This time, we moved away from German shepherds to collies.

Progress was good. We were more experienced now, and training was easier than the first time round, partly because we had been able to train the younger pair of dogs with the two qualified dogs. We were on familiar ground, knew all the pitfalls, and felt certain we would have the dogs qualified in a much shorter time than Dex and Rizzo. My trainee dog was Eiger, a young, black retriever-collie-cross. I had bought him from a farmer and named him after a mountain in Switzerland.

Don and I had committed ourselves fully to another gruelling two years of training Ben and Eiger, a chaotic time for my family. Even if my children were sick, I still went off with the dogs. If I wasn't out training, I was on a call-out – always out, never at home. It was a time of pure and utter selfishness. Bottom line: I was still obsessed.

Dex was now the only qualified mountain-rescue dog in

the Republic of Ireland, and I nearly lost my day job because of the frequency of call-outs. But if somebody was missing, it was hard to refuse to help. Sometimes, it felt almost like emotional blackmail.

Dog Talk

Dogs tend to be blamed for everything they do wrong, whereas ninety-nine per cent of doggy problems are, in fact, created by the owners' lack of knowledge. Humans cause the problems because people keep applying human thinking and psychology to dogs. We're supposed to be the superior race, but to deal with dogs properly we must think like dogs.

A dog's behavioural problems should be corrected in the first six to eight weeks, because when only eleven weeks old, the temperament and character of a dog are already almost fully set. At that stage, a dog's learning capacity has reached its peak. Scientific research carried out in countries such as Sweden, Russia, Holland and the US shows that the most advanced dog in the world has a level of intelligence equal to that of a two-year-old child, and that a dog will never progress beyond that point – not even a trained dog. From the age of two years onwards, certain things can be explained to children, and they can begin to work things out for themselves, thereby increasing their level of intelligence. The same does not hold true for dogs. A dog possesses an innate understanding and will react instinctively to something, just as it would in the wild with other dogs. But a dog's overall understanding of our human world is limited. Dogs have no sense of language but can understand a tone of voice. When

I was a child, my father told me not to talk too much to the dogs. His advice was spot on and has stood the test of time. Shouting as a means of correction is pointless. It causes the dog to link punishment and anger with the owner. Dogs should never know that their owners are angry with them, but should be able to look on their owners as their best friends, masters, mistresses or pack leaders. The key to training dogs is to let them learn by an association of ideas; for example, if a child touches a hot cooker, the child will connect the pain with the cooker. Likewise, if a dog goes beyond the garden boundaries set by the owner, the dog must connect the punishment with the boundary itself – such as an electric fence – rather than with the owner. The wrong deed the dog is committing must cause the hurt.

One night, a guy came to me with a problematic, fourteen-month-old German shepherd. The dog was uncontrolled and had no manners. He was being reared in a family home of four children and had never been disciplined. The owner was becoming worried. Every time he took the dog for a walk, he lunged at other dogs and people without warning. If the owner went to walk one way, the dog would pull in the opposite direction. I took the dog outside for ten minutes and sorted out this problem simply by walking him on the lead and getting him to the point where he walked ahead without distraction and followed my direction instead of pulling in the opposite way. Once he had done it for me, he did it for the owner, but the owner needs to continue the routine to ensure the dog does not revert to his old ways.

Another guy arrived with a troublesome terrier. He said

that every time he left the dog out of his garden run, he headed straight for his neighbour's garden. He was so fed up with the dog's behaviour that he was thinking of getting rid of him the following week. When I pointed out that he already knew the solution to the problem himself, which was simply to keep the dog in the run, he answered, 'That's cruel!' He told me the measurements of the run, and I assured him that it was big enough for six dogs. I advised him to take the dog for walks, let him loose in the garden only when supervised, and keep him in the run at all other times as a terrier will always ramble.

Another owner had a problem with his seven-year-old cross-bred poodle lunging at other dogs and people. He came to me convinced he would have to put the dog to sleep. The dog was wearing a muzzle, and when I examined it, I found that it was too small – so tight, in fact, that he could barely breathe. His eyes were covered in hair, which meant he couldn't see. Naturally, he was always tensed up as he couldn't even open his mouth, and everything around him posed a threat because he couldn't see what was happening. A bigger muzzle and a haircut would solve the dog's problems.

People themselves are too uptight when it comes to dealing with their dogs, and fail to invest time in finding a way to iron out problems. Training and correction proves most successful when owners are relaxed and take time out to deal with any troublesome doggy behaviour. Most of the time, it boils down to using some common sense, nothing else.

People assume dogs can read their owners' minds. No they can't. But they can read body language. A person's face alone gives off a certain aura and the eyes tell much. When owners give commands, they usually give a flick of the hand or they might raise an eyebrow. Dogs can pick up on these actions.

Usually, dogs sniff around strangers when they appear. Owners should never pull their dogs away as doing so causes the dogs to become wary of the stranger and builds up mistrust. Sniffing comes naturally. When dogs smell each other, they are looking for information. When a male and female dog meet, the female starts flirting, whereas when two male dogs come together, each will go off and do a dribble to mark their territory. They'll make eye contact, give a flick of the tail, and bare their teeth to signal an impending attack.

Never let a dog know that you're afraid. This is hard, especially if you are afraid, as you will give off an odour of fear that the dog will pick up. While you may not be able to prevent that, you can disguise the extent of your fear simply by controlling your body language, mainly by not staring at or watching the dog. When someone who has a fear of dogs arrives at our training ground at Hop Island, I usually walk straight over and give them a dog to hold.

In my eyes, every dog I meet is a potential threat until I know otherwise. But there is no point in becoming paranoid. Common sense tells us that owners are unlikely to walk their dogs in the street if the dogs are potentially dangerous. Unbelievably, ninety-nine per cent of dog bites are down to human stupidity. Don't ever make the first move to befriend a strange dog. Don't ever bend down to pat a strange dog. Let the dog approach and smell you. Avoid eye contact as, in an animal's world, eye contact is a challenge. Avoid smiling at a strange dog as, in a dog's world, the sight of bared teeth signals an impending attack. Children tend to be bitten by dogs more than adults as a child usually approaches dogs all wide-eyed and smiling, with their face almost level with the dog's head, which is an approach that dogs totally mistrust. That said, dogs that have been well socialised with humans and other animals from a very young age will totally accept stares and smiles without reacting negatively. When petting or rubbing a dog, it's important to know how dogs lick each other. They use short, gentle touches, not the long, heavy-handed rubs that we humans inflict on them.

After a total of only one hour of proper training, a seven or eight-week-old puppy should have learned everything it needs to know. Training sessions should always be short – only two or three minutes at a time, and just a few sessions daily. Exercise is not the most important factor with young puppies or young dogs; what it boils down to is the quality of training and not the quantity. It all comes back to the same old mantra – perfect practice makes perfect.

During the initial training of a dog, the owner should not give verbal praise. This should be withheld for a few weeks, and will come naturally at that stage. Owners should only play with their dogs during training time. Dogs find it easier to learn through play rather than being forced to train. Get right down on the floor to play with the dog. It's a good way of bonding. While training lasts, dogs should be constantly rewarded with play and food. Trainers' attitudes to rewarding dogs with food have come full circle. In the 1970s rewarding dogs with food was frowned upon, and went out of practice for about fifteen years; today, it's highly recommended. After training, take away all the toys. If toys are left around, the dog will become possessive of them, and may even bite a child to get hold of them.

Ignore bad behaviour and reward good. If a pup piddles on the floor, wipe it up but don't give out. Usually, the owner is at fault for not letting the pup out often enough. A pup has no bladder control until the age of five months. In the first two weeks, a pup should be let out every thirty to sixty minutes, and every two or three hours after that. But don't walk the pup out. Instead, pick up the pup, place it down outside, and stay there for two or three minutes. Don't say a word, and even when the business is done, don't give any praise. Pick up the pup again, let the pup loose inside, and reward it with a game of ball.

Dogs should only be left to wander inside the house when it suits the owners. A house is for humans, not for dogs, and dogs in a house should be kept in a crate lined with newspaper. The crate comes in especially handy when going out. Dogs can be taken anywhere simply by popping the crate in the car – just like a baby carrier or car seat.

In the garden, dogs should be placed in a long, narrow holding pen measuring a minimum of four feet by twelve feet. They should never be loose in a garden, not only because they might destroy it but also because they may come to regard it as their own territory. Leaving a dog loose in a garden increases the risk of a child being bitten by a dog. If the owner wants to leave the dog loose outside, the child should be brought in. Never let male dogs in particular and young children play together unsupervised. When male dogs become sexually mature – usually between nine months and two and a half years, depending on the breed – they become easily excited. Once they start to be assertive, they look on themselves as being part of a pack. Dogs do not see young babies as a threat, but once babies become more forward in their actions – such as hitting the dog or throwing toys – a dog may view the child's actions as a challenge, and might growl. The owners might then punish the dog for growling. If a dog knocks down an eighteen-month-old child in nappies, the child might squeal and may sound like an injured rabbit to the dog. The dog does not see the child as a human and it becomes prey to the dog, and the dog might drag the child around or attack, even to the point of fatality.

When people buy a dog as a present for elderly people, they tend to buy a small pup. A bigger dog would be better as an elderly person is more likely to fall over a small dog than a bigger one, and there are plenty of older dogs in rescue centres looking for a good home. It's also important to take into consideration the consequences of owning a dog, as elderly people who become dog owners may also become isolated. For example, elderly people may stop visiting relatives or friends if they cannot bring their dogs with them, or may not have anyone at home to take care of the dogs while they are away. They can then become prisoners in their own homes, and miss out socially. Much thought should also be put into buying a pup as a present for a child. Unless the family can provide the pup with proper, long-term care, the idea of owning a dog should be abandoned.

All dog owners must act responsibly at all times, and should never allow their pets to wander and mate with whatever happens along the way. Whether big dogs or small, many misconceptions exist about the difference between breeds. The fact that all dogs are related to and bred from wolves is often forgotten. The safest breed for a family pet is a pure-bred wolf. There is no known record of a healthy wolf attacking a human in the wild anywhere in the world. The reverse is true of wolves in captivity. At a minimum, a wolf needs an acre of space to roam. For years now, I've been thinking about buying a wolf, and recently just missed the boat when a guy in North Main Street in Cork had a pure-bred Canadian wolf for sale. I dilly-dallied over the decision for so long that he was gone by the time I had made up my mind to take him.

Regardless of what breed of dog is chosen, the bottom line is that dogs turn out as good as they are reared. At the end of the day, it all comes down to the owner's knowledge of dogs and how that information is used to properly train and socialise the dog. Perfect practice makes perfect. And yes, you can teach an old dog new tricks. It will take longer than it would to train a pup because old habits are hard to change. But it can be done – dogs are never too old to learn. An episode of the TV series *MythBusters* backs this up: two of the presenters set out to prove wrong that adage about old dogs and new tricks. Adam Savage and Jamie Hyneman each took on the challenge of teaching a seven-year-old Alaskan malamute five new tricks in just one week. The two dogs then competed against each other in a trial. In the exam, Adam's dog CeCe obediently performed all of Adam's commands: to heel, sit, go down, give his paw, and stay put for a certain length of time. CeCe was awarded full marks. Jamie's dog played a blinder, too, until he reached the 'stay' command and refused to remain still for the necessary length of time. Nevertheless, the presenters proved that you can, indeed, teach an old dog new tricks. It's never too late.

The Ministers and the Muzzles

In June 1991 Pádraig Flynn, the minister for the environment, introduced regulations that required certain breeds of dogs to wear a muzzle in public. The regulations applied to the American pit bull terrier, bulldog, bull mastiff, Doberman pinscher, English bull terrier, Japanese Akita, Japanese tosa, Rhodesian ridgeback, Rottweiler, Staffordshire bull terrier and German shepherd. As well as wearing a muzzle, the listed dogs were required to wear a collar inscribed with their owner's name and address, or with the same information on a badge or disc attached to the collar. Only a week earlier, Dex had been awarded a plaque for outstanding achievement at the last German shepherd show at which unmuzzled dogs could be legally exhibited.

Doggy people were outraged by the regulations. Strong opposition was voiced against the minister's inclusion of particular breeds on the dangerous-dog list. Arguments were put forward that many of the listed dogs, especially the bulldog, would face much hardship if muzzled as they perspired through the tongue. One bulldog owner said it was like placing a plastic bag over a dog's head. Others argued that careless owners would not heed these laws, and so they would probably affect only conscientious owners – those who act responsibly by socialising their dogs and never leaving them alone with children. These were the ones who would pay the price.

The Campaign Against Muzzling (CAM) was formed in protest against the minister's legislation. The first action group was set up in Limerick, followed by Cork, Dublin and Galway. Support spread through the country like wildfire. CAM accepted the dangers presented by fighting dogs – such as pit bull terriers and tosas – but criticised the minister for taking the wrong approach to the problem. CAM argued that the existing licensing and registration measures operated by the Irish Kennel Club were good enough to deal with the situation, and recommended that the legislation should be aimed at the owners rather than at the breeds. Seán Reidy, spokesperson for CAM, demanded that the legislation should punish the deed, not the breed. He warned that the minister was not dealing with individual people scattered throughout the country but with a strong, nationwide network of dog clubs. The Irish Veterinary Association and the Irish Kennel Club backed the campaign.

Some owners, in a panic, tried to get rid of cross-bred, listed dogs. Many appealed to kennel owners to take them. Other dog owners whose breeds were not on the minister's list feared that more breeds would be added in due course. The Welsh-based search-and-rescue dog unit – which regularly assisted in search-and-rescue operations in the Republic of Ireland – withdrew its services while the muzzling law was applied to their dogs. It even refused to send over Labradors and other dogs not affected by the ruling. Louis O'Toole of the Kerry Mountain Rescue Team stressed the fact that Ireland could find itself in a very serious situation if there was a disaster here like the Lockerbie plane crash.

Despite the growing support for CAM, the minister failed to respond to any contacts from the group, which had lobbied for the exemption of guide dogs and rescue dogs before the introduction of the legislation. A gathering of funds got underway in anticipation of a High Court action. Within a few days of the introduction of the new law, the minister saw some sense. He granted a reprieve to German shepherds working as guide dogs for the blind and as search dogs for mountain-rescue teams. However, though guide dogs were exempted from wearing a muzzle in public, this immunity was not extended to German shepherd rescue dogs. As a result, Dex was required to wear a muzzle at all times except when working as a search dog. This implied that he was 'dangerous' when on-lead and at my side but 'safe' when off-lead and away from me. Typical Irish solution to an Irish problem!

This was a complete joke. Was I expected to walk Dex into a field wearing a muzzle and then take it off in front of a farmer? If I did that, a farmer would naturally view the dog as being dangerous and was likely to ban us from using his land for fear of an attack on his sheep. In light of the high level of training Dex had received, I refused to muzzle him at any time, and felt compelled to withdraw him from carrying out search-and-rescue operations. Officials at Pádraig Flynn's department promised to review Dex's situation with regard to the muzzling law. But time moved on and the law still stood. During this period, I received phone calls from the secretary of the Department of the Environment pleading with me to reverse my decision about not going on search-and-rescue missions.

In February 1992 Mary O'Connor of Blackpool in Cork became the first dog owner in the country to be prosecuted under the new law. She had been walking her unmuzzled German shepherd towards the Glen when a garda stopped her. On the day of the hearing, Dex and I joined a large group of protestors outside the courthouse in Washington Street in Cork. I stood with an unmuzzled Dex at my side and a placard in my hand rejecting the minister's new, and, in my opinion, unjust law. Mary O'Connor was fined £15, which she paid even though the judge acknowledged that she did, indeed, look after her dog, and that she had trained him well.

In the coming weeks, harsh as it may seem, I refused to let Dex search for a man missing in Connemara. Instead, Neil's collie Pepper was brought down from Northern Ireland to look for him. As collies were exempt from the muzzling legislation, Pepper could work without a muzzle. At the time, I said that unless Dex was granted total exemption from the muzzling law, he would not be helping in any future rescues. I was furious. All we were hearing from the Department of the Environment was that dog controls were under review. It was now August 1992 and the whole affair had been dragging on for over a year, with no resolution. I had to take a stance. It would have been impossible for me to carry out a search with a muzzled dog and trying to do so would have caused great hardship to Dex. The search might last for hours and Dex might overheat, or find it hard to breathe. Also, the muzzle would prevent him having a drink of water. As it was likely that the muzzle would become entangled in branches, particularly in dense undergrowth, it might be hard for me to find Dex, since he would have worked by ranging ahead on his own, and he might have been left to die. Going on strike with Dex had gained the attention of the media. RTÉ radio contacted me to give interviews to David Hanley and Marian Finucane. I agreed, and received a gruelling over my strike action on both *Liveline* and *Morning Ireland*. I explained that it was the government that was preventing me from going out to search, and I stressed the fact that I was a responsible dog owner and had trained my dog to a high level. Why would a responsible dog owner walk the streets with a potentially dangerous dog?

Overall, the media response to my action was bad. One newspaper reporter wrote, 'who does Mick McCarthy think he is putting children's lives at risk and playing God with people's lives?' No mention was made of the fact that I was a responsible owner – and an unpaid volunteer – being punished for the irresponsible actions of others.

Months went by, and then the new Minister for the Environment, Michael Smith, was due in Cork. I decided that I would walk an unmuzzled Dex through Cork city on the day of his visit so as to highlight the ridiculous nature of the ruling regarding Dex and to give the gardaí the opportunity to enforce the law. I needed to bring the issue to a head, and I told the gardaí beforehand of my plan. I was only doing what I had always done, as for many years I had walked Dex through the city every Saturday afternoon. As part of his ongoing training, it was important for him to mix with people in a social setting and to feel comfortable in public places. It was vital that he wasn't restricted.

The sun was shining as I strolled into Patrick Street with Dex and stood in front of Eason's. A garda soon arrived and stood beside me. When I explained to him that I had no choice but to make a stand, all he said was, 'Okay.' Other people came along and stood with me in support. Many of them were total strangers. Having stood there for some time, Dex and I then walked up Patrick Street to Daunt Square, and into Grand Parade. Believe it or not, halfway up through Oliver Plunkett Street, Dex left a present of the biggest parcel ever, which I can tell you I cleaned up fast with the help of a local pet-shop owner and some disinfectant. And, boy, was I glad that a photographer was not around to capture the moment.

Within only about a week of my Patrick Street demonstration, it was announced that the muzzling law regarding Dex and other search dogs was to be overturned. Search-and-rescue dogs were to be subject to the same exemption as guide dogs, and also were to be exempt from the licence fee. Paying for the licence had never been an issue, and those of us with qualified dogs decided that availing ourselves of this exemption would be to milk the situation entirely, which we had no intention of doing, so we opted to continue to pay the dog-licence fee. I might add that a dog licence should be cheaper for neutered pets as this would encourage owners to act responsibly. The licence should only be issued upon presentation of a vet's certificate confirming that the dog has been neutered, micro-chipped and vaccinated.

From what I have seen over the years, the gardaí rarely reproach owners when they don't have a muzzle on their dogs. Once the dogs are under control, the gardaí seem happy enough. Usually, dogs only pose a threat in public if they are not socialised or trained properly, and unsocialised and unsupervised dogs create most problems.

But at least Dex was now fully exempt from the muzzling law, and we could concentrate once again on what we were trained and qualified to do – search for missing persons.

The German Boy Scout

One summer in the early 1990s, a German Boy Scout was reported missing on a Donegal mountain. Neil Powell got the shout around 4 p.m. while visiting his parents in Cobh. When he called me at work, my heart started racing. From that moment on, everything went into overdrive. I hurried home to Knockraha to collect my gear and Dex. With my heart still thumping, I drove back towards the city to meet up with Neil and Pepper at the Tivoli roundabout. We wanted to get to Cork airport as fast as possible. Neil put on his blue flashing light, which all SARDA members are entitled to have, as we were now facing into heavy, rush-hour traffic.

As we left the city behind and drove up the airport hill, Neil told me that the missing boy had already spent one night lost on the mountain. Other than that, he knew very little. Always, only the minimum of details are given with the shout. We would have to wait for the briefing to hear the full story.

At the airport, we were ushered quickly through to the runway, where a government jet was waiting for us. We boarded at 7.40 p.m. The aisles of the plane were covered in plastic to protect them from the dogs' hairs. Our pilots were Lieutenant Donal O'Shea and Lieutenant Brian Dunne, two kind gentlemen who had prepared food for us to eat on the journey and packed lunches for the search.

We landed at Finner Camp air strip in Donegal and were then flown by helicopter to the GAA pitch in the village of Carrick. From there, we went by garda car to a remote farmhouse near Slieve League, where we received the official briefing. All information was vital but we were particularly interested to know the age of the boy, his level of fitness and the colour of his clothing. By then, the gardaí had gathered background details of the case. They told us the Germans had been regularly sending plane loads of Boy Scouts to Ireland to carry out soldier-like training. The youngsters came without any money and were expected to scavenge and live off the land, although they were not allowed to kill. Normally, they split into groups of eight to ten, and each troupe chose its own route. On the day before, at 5.30 p.m., one such group had arrived in Glencolumbkille in south-west Donegal. They decided to set off on a horseshoe walk around Slieve League, which they believed would be a safe and easy exercise. The troupe consisted of eight Scouts; their leader was only sixteen years of age.

During the climb, one of the Scouts – an eleven-year-old boy from Hamburg – complained that he was suffering from stomach cramps and refused to go any further. Leaving some of their gear with him and promising to return for him later, the rest of the group carried on. However, on their descent they failed to locate him, and it was not until 1.30 p.m. the following day that the leader of the group reported to the gardaí in nearby Carrick that the boy was missing. A massive air-and-land search got underway. The Scouts firmly believed they had left the boy in a particular spot near a stream, but having scoured the area, the searchers found no trace of him there.

Darkness was setting in when we reached Slieve League. Tensions were running high as fears were now growing that the boy had fallen from the cliffs on the opposite side of the mountain. Searchers had come from everywhere – over a hundred volunteers turned up. A garda superintendent was in charge of co-ordinating the various search teams, which included the Killybegs Coast and Cliff Service Unit, the Shannon Marine Rescue Centre and An Garda Síochána. The Air Corps and British Royal Navy came and went, flying searchers to and from the scene.

The night was dry but freezing cold. Could the eleven-year-old survive a second night on the mountain in sub-zero conditions? Would the Boy Scout skills he had learned back home in Germany help protect him from the elements? Had he stuck with the Scouts' basic rule of staying put when lost, or had he moved? The youngster's chances were looking slim, but we approached the situation with a very positive attitude, believing that we would find him alive.

We double-checked our gear and prepared to begin our search. A local farmer's teenage son acted as our guide. He showed us the areas already searched, and we combed them again. Then we moved on, scouring the rugged, heathery terrain of the most dangerous mountain in south Donegal. By now, Neil and I were the only human searchers left on the mountain. All of the other searchers had been sent home. Eliminating them from the scene would make it easier for the dogs to locate the boy, as their human scent would no longer be present on the mountain. Air-scenting dogs pick up every human scent in a given area, whereas bloodhounds hunt only for the particular scent of the missing person. But there were no bloodhounds available to us. Locating the boy could take hours. There was no time to waste.

Our dogs ranged up to a half-mile away from us. Every now and then, when the lamps on their collars shone through the heather, we could pinpoint their location. We knew they were working well. Dogs search best in the dark as they work with their noses, not their eyes, and can detect scents a mile away or up to five miles in certain conditions. Air-scenting dogs work almost as well in daylight but can occasionally be distracted by other animals or humans. In the dark, they are totally focused.

Hours passed without the slightest hint of progress. We were becoming increasingly concerned. The boy had been missing for nearly thirty-six hours. The treacherous cliffs nagged at our minds, reminding us of their thousand-foot drop into the Atlantic Ocean. But we remained optimistic. Searching with the conviction that the missing person will be found alive helps focus the mind, gives that extra drive, that zip and essential sense of urgency.

At 4.30 a.m. Neil suggested we move over the ridge to the back of the mountain, which was the opposite side to that identified by the Scouts as the location in which they had last seen the youngster. Time was moving fast, and we were aware that the other volunteers would return at first light. If they came back while we were still searching, they would have to wait in the farmyard. Although our dogs are trained to work with multiple handlers at the same time, and will do so ahead of line searchers, there is always a chance that the dogs can be put off by searchers inexperienced in dealing with search dogs. Time-wise, we were under pressure, but we pushed on, determined to find the boy.

Neil and Pepper searched upwards from the bottom. Dex and I worked downwards from the top. After just a further hundred yards, we would be finished with that particular area and switching to yet another part of the mountain. Suddenly, I heard Pepper indicating far below. Neil contacted me on the radio. At that stage, he was about a quarter of a mile below Pepper. Neil suggested I send Dex down to confirm Pepper's indication. Dex made his way downhill, turned left, headed towards Pepper and indicated. Both dogs stood together facing a gully about fifteen feet deep and twenty feet wide, with a sheep fence on top. They cleared the fence, went further in, and kept indicating. Daylight was breaking. Neil and I could see various items in front of us: a guitar, pots and a frying pan. We could see no trace of the boy. But the dogs continued to indicate vigorously.

Then we found him. He had been lying in knee-deep heather, only about three or four feet away from us. We had to walk within a foot of him before he became visible. No wonder we couldn't see him – he was dressed in camouflage, which blended in with the heather, and he was fully concealed in the foliage. Somebody must have been praying for us. There was no way anyone could have spotted him without literally walking over him. More than likely one of the helicopters had flown above him at some point but had failed to see him because he was so well hidden. The other members of his troupe seemed to have misread their position on their descent and arrived at the wrong side of the valley floor.

The boy was unconscious and suffering badly from hypothermia. We gave him some of our clothes, a little piece of a Mars bar and a few sips of water. Having notified base that we had found the boy, we began to carry him down the side of the mountain through knee-deep heather and bogland. This was not an easy task. Although the lad was now awake, he was totally helpless, and even though he was only eleven years of age, he was six feet tall. The farmer's yard, which was the base for the search, was a ninety-minute walk away. Every few hundred yards, we stopped to give the boy a little water. We had almost reached the farmyard when we saw two jeeps full of young, handsome British army personnel approaching. All of them were dressed in dark navy and looked extremely fit. They had not been notified that the boy was found, and had come to help.

At the farmyard, an ambulance was waiting to take the boy to Letterkenny General Hospital, where he was given a thorough check-up and later enjoyed a good Irish breakfast. Having spoken to the boy, the gardaí said the youngster was unable to tell them very much, possibly due to a combination of his thirty-six-hour ordeal and the fact that he spoke very little English. The lad was lucky to be alive; medical sources were quick to point out that he would not have survived another forty-eight hours on the mountain. But despite his experience, he was said to be in excellent condition.

The German Boy Scouts had many lessons to learn from the incident, such as the seriousness of not reporting immediately that the boy was missing. The importance of wearing bright clothing on a climb cannot be emphasised enough, but I've noticed that even our own Irish Boy Scouts tend to ignore this basic rule for hill climbers and walkers.

After the rescue, all of those officially involved in the search disappeared, without offering to get us home. Neil and I, along with Pepper and Dex, were left stranded in Donegal without any means of transport back to Cork. Being left at the side of the road to find our own way home was in total contrast to how other countries look after volunteers: when I was placed on the Welsh mountain-rescue list of volunteers, the Royal Air Force offered to fly me over and back in the event of any call-out.

Being left high and dry in Donegal opened our eyes to the fact that, where possible, it was best to travel to the search area in our own transport; at least we'd be sure of getting back home again. Luckily, a member of a local search team came along and took us back to his house to shower and eat. Then he drove us to Sligo airport. From there, we flew by cargo plane to Dublin, and were then flown free of charge to Cork, courtesy of Aer Lingus. On our return to Cork airport, Ted McCarthy of the *Cork Examiner* photographed us. Over the coming days, we received much media coverage for the rescue, and, as always, Pepper and Dex took it all in their stride.

Without doubt, the rescue stands as an example of cross-border co-operation. Yet while it was common for North and

South barriers to come down in times of crisis, usually such cross-border activity was kept low-key to avoid antagonising militant groups. Even the locals refrained from mentioning such help in the aftermath, even though this cross-border co-operation worked both ways, with members of An Garda Síochána also crossing the border to help out in similar circumstances. The success of the rescue also shows the importance of calling in search-and-rescue dogs early.

In many other countries, such as Britain, Germany and France, police and civilian dog handlers train together to the same standard. Ideally, all search-and-rescue dogs, whether civilian or not, should be certified to the same standard. Even though I have offered to supply, train and livestock-proof search dogs free of charge for An Garda Síochána, the offer has not been accepted. That offer was originally made in 1999, and has stood since then and still stands today. In other countries the professionalism of the volunteer is acknowledged. But the Irish psyche tends to view the volunteer as the amateur and the paid person as the professional, regardless of training, qualification or proven record.

As a society, we need to open our eyes to the fact that when people receive full-time pay for a particular job, this does not necessarily mean that they are more competent and professional than the amateur. When it comes to dogs, the opposite can be true as the amateur tends to be just as passionate about their dogs as the professionals and often even more so.

Nightmare at Wellington Terrace

Searchers can only search the areas given to them by those in charge of the search. This restriction presented me with a near-miss situation in one of the most shocking cases of missing persons in Ireland. In the 1990s three men mysteriously vanished from Cork. Detectives believed they were murdered, and the wheels were set in motion for a huge garda manhunt. All three disappearances were linked to a house of flats near the city centre. But where were the remains? Rumour had it that all three bodies had been dismembered and divided out in plastic bags among a group of people so as to implicate them all in the murders, and so silence them.

The first of the three men – a forty-two-year-old Welshman who had been renting accommodation at 9 Wellington Terrace – disappeared in late April 1994. A few weeks later, a twenty-three-year-old student from Wexford, who worked as a volunteer with the Cork Simon Community, also vanished. It was thought that he had been searching for the missing Welshman. Then, months afterwards, a thirty-four-year-old man disappeared. He had also been living at 9 Wellington Terrace. Later, his sister said that her brother had witnessed the killing of the other two men in the rented house at Wellington Terrace, and that he had been too scared to go to the gardaí and sign a formal statement about the murders. But he had said the murderer was a forty-two-year-old man who had also lived in the same house of flats at Wellington Terrace, and who came originally from Mayfield.

Rumours about the missing men were gathering pace. One story said that the disappearance of the third man was linked to a row over compensation money he received from a road accident in which he lost an eye. Another said he was killed because he was about to spill the beans on the murderer of the other two men. Other accounts connected the killings to a drugs party of about twenty people that was held in the Mayfield area of the city.

In 1996 one of the three bodies was reported to have been buried and dug up again in a field between Mayfield and the Vienna Woods Hotel. The search intensified and media reports were rife that special search dogs were about to be brought in. At that time, I had two certified search dogs: my German shepherd, Dex and my retriever-collie-cross, Eiger. When the shout came, I took them along, with the intention of working each one separately.

Having been briefed at Mayfield garda station, we set off to begin the search in the company of two gardaí. They took us uphill behind the Vienna Woods Hotel, which is located on the verge of the city, high above the roadway and near the village of Glanmire. They led us into a field covered in stubble, and asked us to begin our search there. I explained to the gardaí that if the dogs came across the scent of a buried body, they would react differently. Dex would go straight into the middle of the scent cone, bark at the ground and start digging. Eiger would rush in, jump suddenly, run away and lie down, just as he had done on the Castleisland call-out when the farmer's body was found at the top of the mountain.

We began by searching along the perimeter of the field. Then we combed through the centre. We moved on to a second field, started at the edge again, and worked outwards until we covered every inch. When we entered a third field, one of the gardaí paused, and said to me, 'Do this field carefully.' That was odd. Why would he single out this particular field? We had searched thoroughly through the other two. What was so different about this third field? It was clear the garda knew what was about to happen, but he said no more.

I held Eiger back as Dex started to work from the left to the right of the field, over and back in a zigzag, searching from one ditch to the other. Only minutes later, he began digging in an area just three hundred yards from where we were standing. I told the gardaí he was indicating a dead body. Normally, I'd go up to examine the area of indication. But I refrained, as I wanted Eiger to go instead. I called Dex back. He didn't want to come. I had to roar at him to make him obey. He returned but was still very anxious.

I then let Eiger off. Would he confirm Dex's indication? He ran straight up towards the spot, full of enthusiasm. Once he came within thirty feet of the area, he leaped into the air and dashed back forty yards to lie down. He wasn't at all happy.

What was beneath the ground? Was it the body of one of the three missing men? If so, which one? Or had all three bodies been buried there? Would the rumours about dissecting the bodies prove true? Why had the gardaí brought us here if they already knew what to expect? I didn't know. Questions were still racing through my mind when one of the gardaí turned to me and said, 'That's actually where one of the bodies was buried. It was dug up from there last night.' So the reports were true. Someone had moved one of the bodies. I waited to be told the identity of the body. But the gardaí held tough.

If I'd had the use of a bloodhound at that time, anyone who had walked back home from the burial spot could have been tracked down by their scent. There would have been no escape. I still couldn't fathom why the gardaí had brought us up there. Were they merely testing my dogs to see if they were any good? Or were they expecting to find other bodies in the area?

We walked back downhill towards the hotel. On our way, a big patch of rough ground in another field caught my eye. Even though the field was overgrown with brambles and briars, I could see a path running through it. I was more than familiar with the area, and I knew that the pathway led to the road veering up to the left just after the Silver Springs Hotel. I asked, 'Could we search up there?' The gardaí wouldn't hear of it. They were insistent about where we should search, and I had no say in the matter. It was their call and they decided we should move on to the Slob, an area of sandbanks located at the back of Glanmire village and in front of a grotto. They must have suspected that body parts might be buried there. I feared we might sink on the sandbanks, but they were firm enough to hold us. We combed through there until dark but found nothing. Our part in the search ended and we were not asked to resume it.

Only two days later, a man out strolling with his dog came across a body in the bushes of a field at Lotabeg, an area between the Silver Springs Hotel and the Vienna Woods Hotel – the same area the gardaí had refused to let me search. The dog had wandered into the bushes. When the owner followed, he actually stepped on top of the body, which was lying on the ground. The dismembered, partially burned remains were identified as those of the third victim. Fragments of clothing and dental records helped to make the identification, together with evidence of skull and eye surgery that he had undergone following his road accident. The acting coroner could not establish the time and place of death.

The man previously named by the deceased as the murderer of the first two men to disappear was charged with the murder of the third victim. The post-mortem details of the killing matched the descriptions given by a court witness, who said the accused had mutilated the body. But in 1996 the case was thrown out in the Central Criminal Court when Mr Justice Barr ruled that the accused had been deprived of a fair trial because vital case documents had been withheld. Although he was still the sole suspect in all three killings, he was never charged again. According to newspaper reports, the gardaí believed other people may have helped him to dispose of the bodies.

In May 2003 the suspect committed suicide at his home. The bodies of the first two victims were never found.

Hungry Hill

One of my daughters had a boyfriend from Castle-townbere. When we were invited to his parents' house for tea, I decided that we should make the most of being in the beautiful Castletownbere area and climb a local mountain first, just to whet our appetites. Marie, my daughter Michelle and I set off early in the morning, with our sights set on climbing Hungry Hill, the highest hill in the Beara Peninsula and so named, according to the locals, because of its great hunger for bodies. We drove down beyond Bantry to Eyeries, and parked the van close to the mountain, which is well known for the magnificent views it offers of Cork and Kerry, its scattered outcrops, and the fact that many climbers easily go astray there.

On the day, visibility was poor as a mist hung over the mountain. Even so, I expected that we would finish off the walk in less than four hours, with no bother and in plenty of time for tea. With the help of my map and compass, we climbed nice and sprightly, without any difficulty. Only ten minutes from the top, the sun burst through and the clouds began to disappear. But the mist still shrouded the valleys beneath us. Being almost on top of the mountain with the mist below felt like being on a plane, when only the clouds are visible beneath and look like a sea of candy floss or balls of cotton wool piled one on top of the other.

Within only a matter of minutes, the temperatures seemed to soar. We became extremely hot – so much so that Michelle took off her sweatshirt to allow some sun to her arms and back. As she was very fair-skinned, I suggested she should cover up to avoid getting sunburnt, but Michelle – being a recently qualified nurse and having the arrogance of youth on her side – replied that she knew exactly what she was doing. That was the end of that conversation.

By now, my wife – who was always very fit – had forged ahead and was shouting back at us, 'Hurry up you two.' I put up a bit of a sprint then, making the gap wider between Michelle and me. Marie and I had almost reached the top when Michelle came running up to us screaming, 'I've been stung by a wasp!' I tried to calm her down but to no avail. I was the one to blame, she said, because I was the one who insisted on climbing the hill in the first place. It was all Daddy's fault. Tempers became a little frayed, so I promised we'd be down soon enough, and then we'd be able to deal with the sting at her boyfriend's house.

Because I had been sure that the hill climb was going to be a doddle – just like that torturous day when Don and I climbed the Hag's Glen with the schoolteacher – I never bothered to bring along any food or water. Bad mistake. I'd broken one of the golden rules and I knew it very well. The members of the Kerry Mountain Rescue Team had drilled it into me repeatedly: never venture onto the hills without being properly prepared for any eventuality. I knew all the rules backwards, all the necessary precautions, but had foolishly decided to ignore my training.

At the top of the mountain, I took a compass reading, then packed away my map and compass. Because of the fiery discussion between the three of us over Michelle's sting, I lost my bearing – totally. Then, in the heat of the moment, I made the decision to go off in a particular direction, confidently assuring Marie and Michelle that our van was parked below us, just behind the trees.

I remembered all the times when I was out training on the mountains and stopped climbers who had no supplies or gear to ask, 'Are you okay? Do you know where you're going?' Now, here we were without any supplies and no idea of our location. Marie suggested that I take out my map and compass again to check the bearing. But I was adamant that I knew exactly where we were going, and I told her that we'd be back to the van in less than an hour – words that came back to haunt me later.

We walked on, with Marie occasionally questioning if in fact I really did know where we were going. After a while, I began to doubt my own judgement, but still I continued with the pretence that I knew we were heading in the right direction – stubborn to the last. Having walked for about six hours, I began to realise that we were hopelessly lost. So I eventually gave in and took out my map and compass. It took me a little while but by using some landmarks I managed to pinpoint where we were. Unfortunately, it most certainly was not where we were supposed to be.

At the time we didn't have a mobile phone, and Michelle was becoming increasingly upset that her boyfriend would be worried about why we were so late. We all got into another heated argument then. I reasoned with the two of them that it was easier to keep going than turn back. By now, I had realised that instead of completing a short horseshoe walk, we had, in fact, walked in a straight line right across the mountain. We carried on walking. Eventually, we saw a valley beneath us with some houses and a lake, which I recognised as Glandore Lake. I was familiar with the valley as I had trained there several times with the dogs, and it was a huge relief to find some familiar ground.

We descended to the valley floor and found the roadway leading out of the valley. We were all very tired, hungry and thirsty. The two girls plonked themselves down on the roadside and refused to go any further. I decided to walk on alone and try to get some help. As I walked down the roadway and on past the lake, I spotted two women and some children playing near the lake shore. I approached the women and explained my predicament. But out of embarrassment I lied a little. By this time, I knew where we were in relation to the van, and just could not bring myself to tell the truth. I pretended that we had intended walking over the mountain and back by road to our van but that it had taken longer than we expected. I asked if anyone had a car to take us back by road to the van. When I explained where I had parked my van, they both laughed. I doubt if they believed my yarn as they asked if I realised that my van was at least fourteen miles away, over the Healy Pass!

One of the women hopped into her Mini Minor and gave me a lift back, and during the journey we discovered that we had a mutual friend living in Fermoy who had actually recently donated a pup to me for search and rescue. What a small world! At times, I thought we wouldn't make it over the Healy Pass as the little car struggled on some of the hills, but eventually we did – was I glad to see my old van.

Having thanked the kind woman, I drove back to Glandore Lake to collect Marie and Michelle. We were now under pressure as Michelle was on duty at midnight, and we had to head back to Cork immediately. On our way, we stopped at a phone box to contact Michelle's boyfriend and explain what had happened. He had found our van and realised that we had gone up the mountain. As the day went on, he began to panic and made up his mind that he would contact the gardaí at midnight if there was still no sign of us. We drove on as quickly as possible, and arrived outside the Mercy Hospital in Cork at just five minutes to midnight. Michelle was exhausted, and had to face a twelve-hour shift before getting the chance to have a rest.

But our memorable day on Hungry Hill taught me some very valuable lessons. No matter how experienced you are in climbing, never be arrogant about your abilities to find your way out of trouble on the hills. Use and trust your map and compass. Always take sufficient gear and food regardless of how short your walk may be, and leave a route map on your windscreen. Today, there should be no excuse for anyone getting lost on a mountain, especially now that we have the use of the Global Positioning System – a neat device the size of a pack of cards that can show a climber's exact position on a mountain. Even before setting off, climbers can now download all mountain routes and mark out the path they intend to take. Of course, every climber should still carry a map and compass, and be well up on how to use them.

With hill climbing, one thing is definite: the hills, no matter how small and innocent they may appear, and the weather show no mercy, not even if you're only stopping off for a doddle of a climb on the way to your daughter's boyfriend's home for tea!

Frolics on Caroline Street and Beyond

Search and rescue is a serious business. But working at the glass company balanced it because my workmates were always up for a laugh, just like my uncle, Danny Gleeson, who was a consummate prankster.

At some stage or other, all of my uncles emigrated to England for work. My uncle Danny, my mother's brother, went there in the early 1950s. When, some years later, he returned home to Knockraha for good, he brought back with him a load of gadgets, including a microphone, which looked like a large mug and from which he could project his own voice out through the wireless, or radio, as we call it today.

My grandmother's house was situated in a laneway close to the village church, and every Sunday morning after Mass, a crowd of locals gathered there for a chat, a cup of tea and a listen to the radio. It was their only way of meeting up, and many of them were related. Among them was Larry Maher, father of Tommy Maher, who runs Maher's sports shops. At one particular Sunday morning gathering, Uncle Danny decided to strike.

The crowd was chatting away in the front room, with the radio blaring at full blast in the background. Uncle Danny positioned himself in the parlour. In one hand, he held his imported microphone – which he had already plugged into the radio with a long wire – and in the other he had a speech he'd written about Larry Maher. By then, all of us children had been hunted from the front room as we were not allowed to stay in the same room as the adults. We were in on the act, and stood looking up in awe at Uncle Danny, bursting with excitement. In our humdrum lives, where every day and week was the same, this was a huge event.

In the midst of all the talking, the crowd happened to hear Larry Maher from Knockraha mentioned on the radio. They stopped the chatter immediately and silence fell on the room as the gathering tuned in to hear Uncle Danny – pretending to be part of a news broadcast – spinning some outrageous yarn about Larry. Everyone was taken aback, none more so than Larry himself, who stood there in the middle of the group, open-mouthed, totally puzzled, baffled and enraged by the lies being aired about him. But nobody recognised Uncle Danny's voice, and everyone was convinced that they were listening to a genuine newsreader.

There was holy murder. The whole crowd turned on Larry and interrogated him as to why he had never mentioned the contents of the radio report. They quizzed him left, right and centre. Poor Larry shook his head, and kept repeating in his native Tipperary accent, 'I don't know anything about it!' But his answer didn't appease the mob. They were now even more annoyed, full sure that Larry was withholding information from them. They were out for his blood.

To avoid a punch-up, Uncle Danny had to abruptly abandon his live radio broadcast, dash into the front room, and admit that it was all a practical joke. But nobody was buying it. He had to run back out again to the parlour, collect the microphone, and show them how it worked before he eventually succeeded in persuading them that it was all a wind-up. In only a matter of minutes, he had almost started, and barely averted, a civil war.

If there was a local concert being run, Uncle Danny was sure to appear. He was a fine singer, and, like Neil Powell during training weekends in Wicklow, loved to sing funny songs, such as Slim Dusty's 'The Pub with no Beer', a song he sang so often that I can remember every word to this day. But no matter what he sang, his audience hung onto his every word. He could fire them up with a powerful rendition of 'Seán South from Garryowen' or reduce them to tears with 'Noreen Bawn'.

In those days, owning a car was a novelty, and Uncle Danny cut a dash as he drove up and down the village in his small, one-door, three-wheel bubble car. It looked like something from a cartoon, with one wheel to the front, two to the back and the door lying above the front wheel. The mere sight of the car brought a smile to all the villagers, not only because of its funny shape but also because anyone wanting a spin had to step up the front to get inside, as it had no doors at either side. Uncle Danny always parked the car in my grandmother's laneway. One day, I was lying down on the ground when the car took off, with Uncle Danny inside, and rolled over my legs. But it was so light, it didn't leave a mark.

Uncle Danny was a cheerful, fun-loving character, and people loved him for his good humour, which he never lost, least of all when the chips were down. Even when he was lying at death's door in his hospital bed, having suffered a heart attack, the doctors and nurses couldn't get over the fact that he was still slagging them off and cracking jokes right up till the very end.

In the glass company, we had plenty of pranksters, but few could outdo Denis Galvin, the father of Ricky, who is well known in the tyre business in Cork city and also on the showband scene. When it came to playing tricks, Denis was a master, just like Uncle Danny. He worked with us as a driver and glass packer. In appearance, he was bald and had a glass eye. He was an out-and-out gentleman, very well read and highly intelligent. And he knew exactly which buttons to press when it came to giving the girls in the office the fright of their lives.

The glass business at that time operated from a shop in the middle of Cork's Caroline Street, which is the side street joining Maylor Street to Oliver Plunkett Street. Only a few doors down towards Patrick Street and at the back of Cash's, a coffin maker ran a business supplying coffins to customers from both the city and county. Once the coffin maker finished a coffin, he had a habit of standing it up against the wall outside his shop door, ready for collection or delivery. On one particular day, when the city was covered in snow, he had three coffins lined up outside. Denis Galvin spotted the chance for a wind-up, and decided to make the most of it.

At lunch time, we had an hour and a quarter free, and the girls in the office always headed to the shops for a bit of window shopping. Usually, they'd return in high spirits, arms linked and chatting away. As Margaret Lynch and two other girls from the office were returning after their lunch break, the bold Denis was lying in wait, and as the girls neared the coffin-maker's shop, two of the coffins were still standing upright outside on the pavement. But the third was now flat on the ground, with the lid off. Denis was lying inside, with his hands neatly crossed on his chest. To make himself look even more terrifying, he had whipped out his glass eye.

On that day, I had stayed inside typing up some songs. Denis had already told us of his plan. As the time drew near for the girls to return, we all stationed ourselves upstairs, peering excitedly out the top windows, and waiting impatiently for the fun to begin.

Engrossed in conversation, the three girls came plodding along in the snow. We did our best to hold back the laughter, knowing the surprise that lay in store for them. They approached the coffins, and just as they were passing, the baldy-headed, one-eyed Denis raised himself slowly. 'Hello girls,' he said in a deep, drawn-out voice, before rigidly easing himself back down again. There was pandemonium. The three girls screamed their heads off, and sprinted up the street as if they were taking part in a marathon.

Like Denis, another colleague – with the same name as myself, Mick McCarthy – was a thorough gentleman and also very well read. Mick was a Blackpool man and a great hurler – a megastar in his day. He had played on the same Glen Rovers team as Jack Lynch and had served as a Cork selector. Nobody called Mick by his real name. He was known to everyone as Langton – perhaps because his on-pitch talents matched those of a former Kilkenny hurling captain, Jim Langton, who was later included in the GAA Hurling Team of the Millennium.

Our Langton was always being quoted about hurling matters in the newspapers. He was a mine of information on hurlers down through the decades – going back as far as the 1920s – and could sing off hurling facts and figures as fast as Jimmy McGee. He spoke incessantly about hurling, and people often dropped in to him just to settle an argument on some minor hurling detail. All the hurling fraternity were regular customers of his, and they'd arrive in their droves just to be served by him.

Langton had charge of making frames and framing. People would come pouring in from UCC (University College, Cork) with their scrolls to be framed, and would ask to be served by Langton, who would be called down from upstairs and could be relied upon to charm the lot of them. Langton would engage in a big chat about hurling. Then he'd neatly roll up the scrolls and place them in a drawer. They rarely saw the light of day after that as Langton would forget about them, but he was a great man to come up with an excuse when it came to pacifying a customer. At the time, we used to import material for making frames. One morning, the sinking of a cargo ship featured on the front page of the *Cork Examiner*. Later that day, I overheard Langton saying to a customer, 'That cargo ship that went down in the North Sea, your frame was inside it. Look, there's a write-up about the ship here in the paper.' And he got away with it! Nobody ever had a cross word to say about him even though years after his death customers were still coming in looking for the frames he'd promised them.

While we always had the craic at work, we worked very hard and happily carried out our tasks. We showed a great sense of loyalty to the bosses and to the company. But then the company treated us all very well, too. When I married and needed to get a loan to buy a house, the company signed up as guarantor. At the time, farmer friends were urging me to buy a site out in the country near where I had grown up, which I could have bought for around £200. But times were different then. I wasn't willing to take the chance, and ended up buying a house in the city instead.

When it came to looking for time off for search-and-rescue work, the company always obliged, except during the stint of one managing director, who refused to let me go on searches during the working week. Some of the other volunteers had great difficulty with their employers when it came to call-outs, although certain companies did draw up a deal and gave volunteers a set number of days off each year.

Every day I took off for search and rescue had to come out of my holidays, except in one case recently, where the managing director offered to pay my wages for a week while I went out on a search. If ever I went over the holiday limit, my pay packet was docked. For the first twelve years in SARDA, I used up every single day of my holidays going out on search-and-rescue missions. Not taking a holiday with my wife and family certainly didn't help my marriage, which was already on a downward spiral. The warning signs for a crash landing were flashing before my eyes. But I chose to ignore them completely.

Equinox

At heart, I've always been a loner – always have been and always will be. Give me a day walking in the woods or the mountains with just a dog for company and I'm in heaven – total bliss, without a care in the world. Many times I've said to friends, 'Once I had a guitar, a dog and a tent, I'd happily live in the woods.' But that was all gobbledygook, only macho talk, as I quickly learned when my marriage fell apart and I found myself sinking to the bottom of the deepest, darkest hole of depression, weighed down with loneliness and despair.

All my life I'd spent hours on my own, going off night after night to train the dogs, pounding the roads, and often not returning home until the lights were out and everyone was warmly tucked up in bed. But living on my own was a totally different ball game. I couldn't hack it.

In the early years, when the cracks first appeared in my marriage, I ignored them; I pretended they weren't there. Often, in later years, I tried to repair the damage. I wanted to make a go of it, to hang on in there, not give up without a fight, but at other times I walked away, left it all behind, for short spells, long spells, only to return again, to give it another go, start all over as if we had no baggage, a clean slate. I carried on like that for twelve years, coming and going, unable to make the final break, to walk away forever from my family, my life, my home.

At one point, when we were on the verge of yet another split, I decided to give up the dogs altogether. By now, I was at the top of the pecking order at SARDA, having been involved since we first got together in Laragh way back in 1987. But it was worth a try. I'd nothing left to put on the table, no other card to play. The dogs had to go. They were the ultimate sacrifice. It might be too little too late, but it was the best I could do.

I took a leave of absence from SARDA. By now, Dex had reached old age and was suffering. I knew it was time to put him to sleep and end his pain. I gave my second certified search dog, Eiger, on loan to SARDA. Then I got down to the business of sorting out my difficulties at home. But it proved an uphill battle, with too much water under the bridge and no hope of improvement. Giving up the dogs made no difference. The gel just wasn't there. The writing was on the wall, clear and bright, in big, capital letters and bold print, urging me to make the final move.

I packed up and left, just like I'd done time and time again. But this time was different. I wasn't coming back. After thirty-two years, the marriage was finally over, finished. One evening, shortly after making the final break, I drove out to my mother's house in Riverstown for a chat with my sister about my new-found permanent status. We'd always been very close, and, because we worked together, saw each other almost every day of the year. My mother was out in the backyard hanging out some washing – always on the go, never idle, just like she was when we were kids. We hadn't spoken to each other for years – not since the night my father came home from Carrigtwohill with a Yorkshire terrier she didn't want. She got odd with me over it simply because I was with him when he bought the dog. She hadn't uttered a word to me since, not for fifteen years.

But I was every bit as stubborn as she was, and wouldn't make the first move. I wouldn't cross the line, shake her hand or put the past behind us. In a way, it suited me to keep my distance. Even though I was now a grown man in my fifties, she still scared the hell out of me, and I still half expected her to give me a clatter around the ear.

I was chatting away to my sister, telling her about my situation, when, out of the blue, my mother – referring to my wife – shouted in through the open kitchen window, 'Is that woman at you again, Mikey?' I nearly fell off the chair in amazement. Was that my mother's voice I heard, talking to me, calling me by my name, having disowned me for all those years? Already, she was taking sides, lining up with me, preparing for the fight, even though my wife had always been up and down to her, helping her out in the house almost every day of the year. They were like two peas in a pod when they got together. But it shouldn't have come as a surprise because we all know that blood is thicker than water, especially when the going gets tough.

My sister and I sat there, waiting for my mother's next move. Dressed in her floral apron and armed with her empty washing basket and peg bucket, she came in with the stride of a sergeant major and looked me straight in the eye, as my sister and I stared up at her in awe, still reeling from the shock of hearing her talk to me. By the look of her, you'd swear nothing had ever happened between us – that we'd been best buddies for all those long years of silence. 'There's a place for you here, Mikey,' she said, laying a hand on my shoulder. But pride got the better of me. 'No, Mam. I'll sort it out,' I said.

But it wasn't as easy as I thought.

Living alone came as a shock. I wouldn't wish it on anyone. There are only so many hours you can spend watching television or reading, and only so many times you can walk a dog. Once you have time on your hands, the loneliness factor sets in and drains the life out of you. For a time, I lived in my van – myself and my dog Bob, a collie-mix I'd bought from a local farmer while I was still living at home with my wife and children, having taken a year out from the dogs. When I first set eyes on Bob, he was only twelve weeks old and in very poor condition. He had never been socialised, and he'd had very little human contact during the most critical period in a dog's life, which is from three to eleven weeks. As a result, he was extremely nervous and frightened, even of his own shadow. His left ear was swollen from a haematoma caused by scratching mites in his ear canal; the swelling was the size of a tennis ball. He ended up with a cauliflower ear and had no hearing in it. In the coming weeks, I spent several hundred euros on visits to the local vet, who found that Bob had only partial hearing in his right ear.

From the very start, I took him everywhere I possibly could, including regular trips up Carrauntoohil. He never relaxed except if he was on a mountain or in a forest. Over the following few months, I tried every trick in the book to socialise him, but it looked as if I was going to fail miserably. Deep down, I felt he hadn't a hope of making it as a working dog, or even a pet, as it seemed his temperament was very bad with people and with other dogs. As this meant he could not be passed on to another owner, I began to think of euthanasia as an option. But everyone at home felt very sorry for him. In spite of everything, he was very affectionate and responsive. Marie did basic training with him, such as obedience, and she seemed to be making some progress. So we decided to keep him.

Bob loved to search. On making a find, he'd run back to me and bark furiously. If I dared ignore him, he'd jump up on me and pinch me on the arm. After a training session with Bob, I usually came home with black and blue marks all over my arm. When I left home for good, I brought Bob with me. Now the roles were reversed and I was relying on Bob to save me.

Living in the van was rough, tough, depressing and degrading. But even if I'd had a palace, it would have made no difference: space wasn't the issue. When I moved to a rented house, the loneliness got worse. I hated coming home from work, turning the key in the front door, knowing that the only sound I would hear would be the panting of the dog. I dreaded the long, dark night ahead, every night the same, dragging on and on.

It seemed to me then that Bob was my only friend, my one true, constant, loyal companion. I spoke to Bob as if he was a human – so much so that I felt, some day, he might actually answer me back! I did have friends who called in regularly and tried their best to cheer me up. But as soon as they left, I felt lonely again.

My daughter Michelle was very good with dogs and wise enough to see how much I relied on Bob for my sanity. She also knew that I was big into German shepherds – more so than any other breed – and so she decided that a German shepherd was just what I needed to give me a bit of a lift and pull me through. We drove to a riding centre near Ennis and she bought me Jack. I couldn't believe my eyes when I saw his papers and realised that Jack's father was a great-grandson of Dex, the first dog I qualified in search and rescue, and whom I had recently put to sleep. Jack's father was an Italian-registered dog bought by a friend of mine from Mike Worral in Belgium. When my friend made the purchase, the pet-passport scheme had just come in, and he ended up having to leave the dog in Belgium for some time with Mike. One Saturday, when I was training in Glanmire, my friend called down with this dog, having just collected him from the airport. What an impressive-looking dog: he had a head like a lion and was in a totally different league from what we normally see. Unfortunately, this dog subsequently went through a number of different owners, and the last I heard was that he was working as a guard dog in a hunt kennels. I'd buy him in the morning if I could afford him.

Jack was with me night and day. I brought him to work with me in the van, took him out training in my lunch hour, and left him to sleep in my bedroom at night. If I decided to leave my van door open, I could trust him to stay inside, no problem. But keeping two dogs in a rented house just wasn't on, and I decided to find Jack a new home. He was young and had an excellent temperament, and I knew he would settle into a new home without a bother. I offered him to a club member, Kieran, who was an experienced dog handler and excellent trainer. Afterwards, any time I ever met up with Kieran at training sessions, Jack would hop into my van, expecting to come home with me. Because of the way I had reared him, he was still bonded to me more than anyone else.

The dogs had pulled me through my separation and helped me to survive. And I was lucky because others were looking out for me – those who knew my situation well. Friends from my doggy circle rallied round and started calling to my house. They always came in pairs, usually under the pretence that they were on their way to do a bit of training, and stayed for an hour or two. They were standing by me, keeping a close eye on me, picking me up and trying to make me feel as if I belonged. They filled my house with noise and occupied the empty chairs. Among the pairs of callers was Áine Dorgan, a veterinary nurse with whom I had always been good friends – ever since she first came along to training sessions having read a write-up about us in a magazine. She was laid back, had a warm, open, sunny personality, and was good fun. At the time, she was renting a house in Ballincurrig. During one visit, Áine said to me, 'Why don't you move in with me and rent a room? I could do with sharing the rent.' She was throwing me a lifeline, when I was on my knees and desperate to survive. Pride would not get the better of me now as it had when I refused my mother's offer of help. I gladly accepted Áine's kind suggestion. And so my days of living alone came to an end.

For several weeks, I spent many nights worrying about where I'd end up. As time moved on, I still found it hard to handle my single status. But the loneliness lessened. I stopped taking myself so seriously and learned to laugh again. Then Áine surprised me with a dog for my birthday. She went to Kieran and bought back Jack. He was the best birthday present I ever got! He had never forgotten me and after three years away was back with me again. Kieran had put a lot of time into training Jack during the intervening years and was very reluctant to part with him. However, any time we met, I was constantly telling him how much of a mistake I had made letting Jack go in the first place, so Kieran knew how much I wanted him.

Jack always wanted to be around me, to be taken out for a walk or a run. Any time I took him to training classes, he'd watch me through the legs of other people if I was at a distance. Then, if he heard my voice, he'd come running in between everyone and all the dogs. But there was blue murder between Jack and Bob. They became bitter enemies. If one came near me, the other would start vying for my attention. Many a time I had to tear them apart. I ended up having to train them separately. I could have neutered them but didn't because they were too old for it to be effective. Primarily, neutering prevents dogs from breeding. It can also help them avoid fighting with other dogs for positioning in a pack, as the highest-ranking dog usually gets the female. Ideally, dogs should be neutered around nine months of age, as older, dominant dogs are likely to have fixed habits that neutering cannot eliminate.

The relationship between Áine and myself had moved up a gear: we were now dating. The days of depression and loneliness were left behind. I had a flutter in my heart and a spring in my step, a reason to get up each morning and someone to come home to every evening. I was living again and life was good.

Back to Basics

During my break from search and rescue, the gardaí and other rescue agencies kept ringing me for help in finding missing persons. Of course, I couldn't respond as I no longer had a trained working dog.

Sometime around the opening of the Jack Lynch Tunnel in 1999, a man phoned me for advice on training his German shepherd puppy. The Cork Society for the Prevention of Cruelty to Animals had recommended he contact me. Gary Daly came to my house with his puppy, and we immediately hit it off. When he showed me the pup's pedigree certificate, I found that his pup Zeus was a cousin to Jack and a great-grandson of Dex. I explained to Gary about the types of training, from competition obedience to *schutzhund*, agility, and search and rescue. I pointed out that the basics of the various facets of dog training were initially the same, and showed him some techniques of puppy training. A week later, Gary returned, eager to show off the tricks Zeus had learned. They had both worked very hard, and Zeus responded quickly to several different commands.

As time went by, it was plain to see that Gary was what I term a 'doggy man'. While it's possible to give dog owners the techniques to train a dog to become an obedience champion, only ten per cent of these handlers will ever be doggy men or women. Yes, they're capable of training the right dog to a certain level, but give them a difficult dog with a variety of problems and they are usually stumped, even to the point of stating that the dog is incapable of being trained. I was hugely impressed with how Gary and Zeus continued to progress, and working with them rekindled my love of serious dog training. For the first time since taking a break from search and rescue, I began to feel excited and enthused again. I couldn't wait to get back into the swing of things, and within weeks I was into my old routine of regular training. It was like a new lease of life, and I knew then that this was the only existence that interested me. Dogs were my life and everything else was secondary.

Gary soon began bringing some friends along to training, and from there things started to snowball quickly. I could sense that some of these people were anxious to be part of a more formal group or club, so I suggested we form a search-dog association, and so it was that K-9 Search Dogs came into being. I was not entirely happy about this as I always hoped that I could return to SARDA, but other people had taken my place during my leave of absence and there was no real place for me now in the organisation. I regularly crossed paths with several of the old guard in SARDA, and they always seemed happy enough to talk with me. However, there was never any talk of my returning to the fold. This bothered me a lot as I really felt there were already too many small search-and-rescue associations around. This manifested itself when I would turn up to a shout to be met by many different groups with the same aim: to find the missing person. The problem with this was that they all wanted to be the group that found the missing person, and, consequently, these different groups tended to do their own thing instead of being co-ordinated into one organised search group. The rivalry between many of the civilian groups was obvious at many of these shouts. The rule within our own group, K-9 Search Dogs, was to do our job and go home. Many of the call-outs and finds we have made over the past few years are not even recorded. My attitude generally is this: who cares who makes the find just as long as the missing person is located.

With a formal association in place, K-9 Search Dogs began to train with more intensity. Our purpose was to train dogs to look for missing people, but along the way we wanted to enjoy our dogs, and that was our priority in training. We were not affiliated to any dog teams, although most of us at K-9 were members of the German Shepherd Association, which is itself a member of the International Rescue Organisation, and we thereby automatically became members of that organisation. But we never conformed to its rules, mainly because its methods of training are of little practical use in searches here in Ireland. Also, its standard of obedience and control is very rigid, and we felt that conforming to it would deprive our dogs of the enjoyment we want them to have in training. Very soon, our numbers increased dramatically. Don and Rose Ryan, with their golden retriever, joined us, added some semblance of order and helped keep us in check as they were both excellent administrators.

During this time, we received a few visits at training from the then SARDA chairman, Noel Murphy. He was having a few misgivings about his dog Holly. He believed SARDA was preventing him from entering his dog in assessments as it felt his dog wasn't ready. It was obvious that he was becoming frustrated, despite the fact that he was chairman of SARDA. Eventually, he asked me if I could help in preparing his dog for an upcoming assessment in which he hoped to take part. I agreed to help, and we began to meet several times each week for training. When work commitments prevented Noel from attending training, Richard Cotter would bring Holly along. Though Richard had no dog of his own, he was an intelligent and competent dog handler. Although Holly ticked most of the boxes required to be a search dog, it was obvious that my mantra 'It's perfect practice that makes perfect' was not being employed. Yet when this changed, Holly very quickly began to make progress. Within a few months, Holly and Noel passed their search-dog assessment and were officially declared an active search-dog team. Noel was thrilled, and phoned to thank us for all the help.

Shortly after this, Noel was voted off as chairman of SARDA, and occasionally began to turn up at some of our training sessions. We had an open-door policy for all dog handlers, so Noel was more than welcome, and we began to invite him along to many of our call-outs. Noel is one of the most knowledgeable people I have ever met. He is a brilliant instructor in first aid and rescue techniques, and had served as an instructor with the Civil Defence for many years. If ever I have an accident, I would prefer Noel to attend above anyone else. He has it all.

Shortly after leaving SARDA, Noel went to work with British Telecom for two years, during which time he trained with SARDA Wales and the Severn Rescue Unit. Training or undergoing assessments with foreign search teams can be challenging, especially if their priorities differ from ours. In one particular qualification test I had taken with Dex in Wales, the assessors were obsessed with the fact that dogs should have a coat on their backs during searches. They were convinced that putting coats on dogs signalled that a search was underway, excited the dogs, and put them in a working frame of mind. Not in my book! During the assessment, Dex was working in a mountainous area of brush and heather, with dense undergrowth and sections fenced off in barbed wire. Working with a coat was impractical as it was likely to get caught in the barbed wire. When I took it off, a radio call came in immediately from one of the assessors. He ordered me to put the coat back on as working without it would hinder Dex's performance, but I did not agree and continued without it.

During the assessment, Dex struck on a scent while walking across a ridge, and went out to the edge of an overhang. For safety, I crawled out on my stomach to check the ground below, only to find there was a drop of about thirty feet to boggy ground beneath the overhang. I checked around but failed to see any body. While I was doing this, Dex became frustrated and decided to jump down. My heart was in my mouth, but when he landed he picked up the scent of the body underneath. Immediately after Dex's jump, another radio call came from the assessor to enquire if Dex was dead. I had to find a way down, which took some time because of the nature of the terrain. I could hear Dex barking his head off in a cave

A handy observing trio: Mick and SARDA UK members in Cumbria
© Mick McCarthy

Bob, the first qualified water-search dog in the Republic of Ireland
© Mick McCarthy

Cassy, Dex, Zoe and Eiger
© Mick McCarthy

Irish Search Dogs, Farran Woods, Co. Cork, May 2009
© Glen Barton

Neil Powell and Mick McCarthy after a successful search for a Boy Scout in Donegal, July 1992. Courtesy of the *Irish Examiner*

Dex on Hag's Tooth Ridge
© Mick McCarthy

Dad, myself (aged 12) with brothers and sisters at The Vee in Riverstown,
Co. Cork, 1963
© Eileen McCarthy

The McCarthy family, taken outside Knockraha church, Co. Cork, 1954:
my parents, John and Mary; (children, from left): Mary Philomena (aged
5), Eileen Maria (aged 8 months), Michael (aged 3½), John Anthony
(aged 8 months), Daniel Joseph Martin (aged 2)
© Eileen McCarthy

Nana Gleeson and Shane
McCarthy, Knockraha,
Co. Cork, 1973
© Eileen McCarthy

On my tricycle in
Knockraha, Co. Cork
© Eileen McCarthy

Shane, Michelle and
Gemma McCarthy,
Mayfield, Cork, 1979
© Mick McCarthy

Mick with Eiger in the front garden, Knockraha, Co. Cork
© Mick McCarthy

Mick with Killarney Mountaineering Club, 'taking it easy'
© Mick McCarthy

Summit of Carrauntoohil, Co. Kerry, Sunday 27 March, 1988
© Mick McCarthy

In Moanbaun Woods, Watergrasshill, Co. Cork (from left): Dex, Cassy,
Elka, Eiger
© Mick McCarthy

Front garden in Knockraha, Co. Cork (people from left): Shane, Michelle, Gemma; (dogs from left): Dex, Cassy, Eiger, Schnauzer
© Mick McCarthy

Diver Paul McCarthy helping out with water-search training along with (dog) Teddy and Mick McCarthy, Farran, Co. Cork, summer 2009
© Glen Barton

Belle (Cáilín Álainn at Andorra Annual Champion 08) on the day she gained her championship title in Cloghran, Dublin, 15 November 2008 © Glen Barton

Mick McCarthy ascending a tricky spot on Carrauntoohil, Co. Kerry, April 2007 © Glen Barton

Mick once again stops
for a chat, while Bob
waits patiently
© Glen Barton

Bob, having
descended a
sponsored climb of
Carrauntoohil, Co.
Kerry, 29 April 2007
© Glen Barton

Harry, trying to be obedient on the agility table, at a Sunday-morning training session, 8 April 2007 © Glen Barton

Caelán and Belle taking it easy on a Sunday morning in the training grounds in Moanbaun Woods, Watergrasshill, Co. Cork, 8 April 2007 © Glen Barton

Jack with Badgershill East of Eden, Eve, as a puppy. She is now owned by Sherry Robertson in the USA © Sherry Robertson

Water-search
training in Farran,
Co. Cork
© Glen Barton

Mick preparing for show Cáilín Álainn at Andorra Annual Champion 08
© Glen Barton

West Cork gardaí welcome west Cork's latest search asset, 16 March 2010 (from left): Glen Barton, Insp. Gerry Lacey, Paddy Harkin, Supt Eoin McEoin, Insp. Brendan Fogarty, Áine Dorgan, Sgt Mick Lyons and bloodhound Karla (now on-call 24/7 for the west Cork region)
© Mick McCarthy

Mick and Glen on their way to a training session in Watergrasshill, Co. Cork, with Harry, Ben and Lucy, 13 November 2009
© Pat Rowe

Kram keeps a close eye on his handler Mark Collings
© Suzanne Collings

It's terrible how the last generation are still having trouble with modern technology (13 November 2009)
© Pat Rowe

Rizzo at Barley Lake; he later died searching on Mount Brandon for a
missing tourist
© Mick McCarthy

Ceo and Teddy – both members of Irish Search Dogs – on their travels
once again: Switzerland, 5 August 2009
© Claire Duncan

7 a.m. on Carrauntoohil, 27 February 2004: just woke up and Derek phones Olga to hear it's pouring rain below the clouds in Killarney © Paul Ramsell

– so vigorously, in fact, that the guy waiting inside said, 'I was afraid to come out.'

Back at base, we had a big discussion on dogs wearing coats. The assessors were amazed that Dex had performed so well despite having had his coat taken off, and that he had dared jump off the thirty-foot crag. I explained to them that he had no fear of heights as we trained at home in sand quarries. What it boiled down to was that the assessors, like most of their European counterparts, were first and foremost mountaineers. They lacked the same knowledge and understanding of dogs that we had as dog handlers. In search-and-rescue operations, whether or not dogs wear coats makes no difference to how they perform. If dogs have drive, they will work regardless of everything else. If dogs don't work when they are not wearing a coat, they are not much good as search dogs. And common sense tells us that dogs with coats swelter in warm weather. In search-and-rescue missions, a dog should only wear a coat if it becomes necessary to let people know that a search dog is at work. In those situations, I'd put a bright orange coat on the dog, with a light attached.

At K-9, the wearing of dog coats never became a condition when I assessed and certified dogs for search-and-rescue work. And if I failed a team, it was only because the handler or dog didn't come up to the mark. The basic requirements of search dogs are that they must be stock-proofed, capable of hunting – like any hunting dog – for human scent, and able to indicate a find to their handlers and lead the handlers back to the source of the find. The obedience required is very basic – merely an immediate return to the handler when called, and some directional control. I have seen many potentially good search dogs ruined by the handlers insisting on too much obedience from their dogs. Really good search dogs wouldn't win any prizes at beauty shows or obedience competitions, and the best search dogs are those bordering on being highly strung and wired. They want one thing only and that's to work, work, work. The most laid-back of dogs can be trained in search routine, but these dogs will give up after a short time working. A search dog needs the fire and drive to work, even when exhausted, as a search may take several days.

Recently, a new member of our Hop Island training group came up to me and asked, 'Why is it that all your trainers' dogs appear so fiery and aggressive?'

We usually tie our own dogs up to the sides while helping new dog owners with their dogs. 'Have you seen any of our dogs attack or jump at other dogs or people?'

'No.'

'Watch,' I said to him, as I went and let my own German shepherd off his lead to run loose among the other dogs and people. 'Now,' I asked, 'does this dog look like he's going to bother anyone?'

He had no reply to this, so I went on to explain the requirements for a really good search dog as opposed to a dog trained just to carry out the routine. To qualify, dogs must be very enthusiastic; they must have fire in their bellies. But their handlers must be encouraging all the way, just like team managers on the sideline at a match. They must constantly bring out the drive in the dogs no matter how tired the dogs become. Handlers must train the dogs over and over again without ever showing any signs of depression themselves. Dogs learn mistakes much easier than the correct training methods. There can be no let-up. Dogs can cover eight to ten miles in an hour, and can become very tired. Handlers must be very vocal and show eagerness in their voice, especially when dogs are ranging out.

A foreign national who was living in Cork had trained with us and had reached the pre-assessment qualification level with her collie. She was a good handler, extremely fit for mountain-rescue work, and could cover ground ten times faster than most. Her dog was excellent. I carried out the pre-assessment in the Hag's Glen – a tough, wild area. The searches were long and hard. The dog worked well, but I couldn't give the OK as the handler was too laid back. At times, she didn't know when the dog had found a body. The dog was becoming tired quickly. His indication was getting weaker. The handler needed to be more passionate, to have the zeal to invigorate the dog and drive him on. She needed to train more, to improve her skills of reading an indication and to develop her enthusiasm. Her problems could be corrected. It was only a matter of putting in the time and staying focused.

Search and rescue is definitely a young person's game. You must be able to get up and go. Everyone is anxious to qualify, to be called out on a search, to feel that buzz. But there are no short cuts, and proper training with the right mindset is the only way. We lost many people who could have gone on to become great search-dog handlers because they were not willing to put in the time. To bring a dog to the qualification stage takes a lot of repetition of the same exercises, over and over again, hundreds of times. A minimum of two thousand hours must be put in, and that excludes travelling. Training sessions should be built up to sixty miles a week. Dogs must be super fit to survive and pass an assessment as they will be required to cover eighteen to twenty miles every hour they work, and this will continue for many hours each day over a period of three to four days. A properly trained, fit dog will fly through the assessment and show no signs of tiredness.

As time went on, K-9 became very involved with the Red Cross – so much so that we eventually decided to disband K-9 altogether. We made a clean sweep and put all our funds and equipment into the Red Cross. But not long after, politicking reared its ugly head among some of the search-dog handlers. Apart from these troublesome few, the Red Cross people themselves were really lovely. I was in a quandary, stuck in the middle. Deep down, I didn't want to leave. But I had no choice: I just wanted to train dogs. It was time to get out, and fast. Áine and I left, and a few more just gave up. We trained away on our own for a while. Then, along with Kieran Murphy from Rylane, we set up Irish Search Dogs. We agreed that we would work without committees or officers. We clear everything with each other but nobody has any title or any degree of control. We have no restrictions on membership. Like K-9, as time went by we had to bend a little to formality and move with the times, which included the setting up of our own website, a task undertaken by Glen Barton. As well as giving a history of the club, the website introduces the dogs, carries a summary of the more high-profile call-outs, and has news on upcoming events. Some of our members have joined the Civil Defence, and are gaining experience in other areas of rescue and first aid.

If any of my adult children went missing in the morning, I'd want the searchers out straight away. But the hands of the gardaí are tied as they have to wait twenty-four hours after an adult is reported missing before they can do anything. It must be very frustrating for the families of missing people when hours and sometimes days pass without any apparent action by the government agencies. This is where the civilian agencies come into play: once they receive a shout, they can immediately begin a search. Emergency response should mean immediate response. Too many rules and regulations tie up search teams and prevent them from responding immediately, and I believe many of these rules and regulations should be removed. If someone is reported missing, do something about it now, not in several days' time. If it turns out to be a false alarm, so what? The fire service answers every call immediately despite the fact that many of these calls are false alarms, so there is no reason why the other services cannot answer calls without delay, and perhaps more people would be found alive. We have too many search organisations pulling in different directions, and that doesn't help provide the service we deserve.

Bothered and Bewildered

A gang of us were doing some light training in a wooded area near Watergrasshill. It was one of those days when I seemed to be just going through the motions rather than taking it seriously. A young foreign national living in County Cork happened to join us for the session. She introduced herself but her name went in one ear and out the other. She offered to act as a body for George, a very young bloodhound with very little training behind him. Poor George couldn't find his way out of a brown paper bag, but he needed a run.

I showed the young woman a boggy area of about a quarter of a mile square and covered in dense bushes. I told her to stay put until George found her. Normally, a handler would always know the exact spot where the body is lying, and would work the dog towards it if the dog failed to find the body naturally. But on this occasion, being as laid back as I was, I let the young woman pick out her own hiding spot within the given area. I made the mistake of not checking where she was, and I didn't even know the general direction she had taken.

An hour went by and then another half-hour on top of that. There wasn't so much as a tickle coming from George. After that length of time, many of the people acting as bodies – especially if they're Irish – would have packed it in. But there wasn't a sign of the woman appearing, and I couldn't go shouting her name because I'd forgotten it. I scoured inside the boundary area again with George, and combed all around outside it. But our luck was out. By now, most of the gang had gone home as they were only puppy training and so their training sessions were short. Then, by pure chance, Gary Daly happened to come along with his trainee dog. Was I glad to see them! I nearly kissed the ground when I saw them coming. As they set off in search of the body, my hopes were high. But like George and me, they failed in their task.

The young woman had been in hiding since 11 a.m. It was now three hours later. There was nothing else for it but to call in the emergency services: Áine and Zak. Of course, Áine let me have it when she found out I didn't even know the woman's name or where exactly she was hiding. Zak always works with great nose and determination. He came in along the path, walked through a gap in the woods, indicated, barked and went straight in. He was spot on with his location. Up popped the young woman from a six-foot mound of heather and bushes with her hands in the air, as if it was a hold-up. God only knows what she thought of us! Being from abroad, I suppose, and new to the training, she had done exactly as she was told and would probably have stayed there all night if it had taken that long for us to find her.

Another time, I was in the middle of a training session with Bob at The Vee in Lismore. Noel Murphy arrived late, around midday. He had been at a party the night before and looked the worse for wear, but he had stuck to the promise that he would turn up and be a body for us. I sent him up the side of the Sugar Loaf to an area about a mile square. 'Don't go too high,' I said to him. 'Just make it a one-hour search.' Usually, we give the body about thirty minutes to get into position.

Bob and I started searching for him. The going was tough. The climb was steep. We had to trudge our way through knee-deep heather all the way up. It was like climbing never-ending stairs with resistance. Four hours later, we were still searching. I kept shouting Noel's name as loud as I could. There was no reply. I tried contacting him on the two-way radio but there was no answer. I was getting very worried. It was now almost twilight. I was seriously thinking about calling in the South East Rescue.

Then I decided to search further outside the boundary area where Noel was supposed to be hiding. We climbed higher still. Bob ranged ahead. As I neared the top of the mountain, Bob disappeared over the summit. Then he indicated. We were now a good half-mile outside the boundary area. I ran up. Bob was barking eagerly down into the heather. Was Noel dead or alive? I feared the worst. But there he was, all snuggled up in his bivvy bag, having a good old snooze for himself. He made absolutely nothing of the fact that he had climbed way above the boundary or that I'd been looking for him for half the day: 'Oh, I just got into a rhythm,' he said, 'so I decided to keep going.' But at least he was safe, and all was forgiven – but not forgotten!

One of Noel's best buddies was Richard Cotter, who was one of a few young fellows who came up from Midleton with Noel to act as bodies for us. Not everyone stuck the pace, but it was no bother to Richard. He came any time we wanted him, and did exactly as he was told, to perfection. He was the ideal body: he was enthusiastic, could entice any dog to run after him, and was a natural with a map and compass. Richard was quiet, a special guy, and he had a wicked sense of humour. Once, when he went on a call-out with Noel for a woman missing in County Limerick, the two of them kept shouting the woman's name as they searched: 'Mary! Mary!' They couldn't find a trace of her, high or low. Later, when they went into a hotel for some food, they saw a poster on the wall about her disappearance and realised her name was Ann. Quick off the mark as always, Richard said, 'No wonder we couldn't find her. We were calling the wrong name all along.' Luckily the missing woman turned up safe and well afterwards.

On another day, Áine and Noel were training with the dogs in a quarry dotted with deep ponds when they were joined by a newcomer and her dog. Áine offered to throw a ball for the woman's dog, but it accidentally landed in the middle of one of the ponds. Áine apologised: 'Don't worry,' she said, 'I'll buy you another one.' The words were barely out of her mouth when the woman began to strip down to her birthday suit before plunging into the water and retrieving the ball. Áine and Noel still haven't fully recovered from the experience – and probably never will.

Water-dog

Neil Powell – a co-founder of SARDA and a man with whom I'd worked on a number of searches – was always testing new ground with the dogs. Luckily for us, his experiments led to the instigation of water-search dogs in Ireland. In 1992 Neil began training a German shepherd named Cuisle as a water-search dog. At the time, Ireland and the UK had no dogs qualified for search work on water. Neil was well at home working on water as he had previous experience with the Royal Navy and had also served as a crew member with the Royal National Lifeboat Institution, a charity set up to save lives at sea.

Cuisle learned how to search for the scent of decay from a person who had died recently or months earlier, and became the first ever water-search dog in Ireland and the UK. His newly acquired skills were first put to the test in the Glenties in County Donegal, where he went out on a boat searching with Neil and a member of An Garda Síochána. He gave a strong indication on one particular spot. When a diver went directly down from there, he found a body at the bottom of the sea, sixty feet below.

Neil has had much success with other water-search dogs, among them Fern. During the Easter holidays of 2007, Fern was involved in the search for the bodies of two teenagers in Castlewellan Lake in County Down. When he made an indication, a member of the Northern Ireland Fire Rescue Service marked it with a buoy. The bodies were later recovered only ten feet from the marker. Fern is also credited with the recovery of a man drowned in the River Boyne at Navan, County Meath, in March 2008. Divers found the man's body lying only fifty-five yards up river from where the dog had indicated.

Neil succeeded in training his dogs to search an area of water stretching to roughly a half-mile square in about an hour, showing an accuracy of ninety to ninety-five per cent in the first sweep, depending on the wind and current, then increasing this detection rate even more in a second sweep. Neil had done all the groundwork and put the rest of us on the right road with regard to water search. Based on what I'd learned from him, I trained away here with Áine, Noel Murphy and our dogs, Holly, Zak and Bob.

Water search is much easier than searching for bodies on land. In water search, a dog's level of concentration is much higher than on land, and its indication in water is also much stronger. But setting up a water-search training session is hard; it takes at least two hours, and the deeper the water, the longer it takes. Also, a lot of manpower is needed. Divers must be on hand, together with a boat, a person to steer the boat and another person on shore. The river or seashore should be at least three feet in depth. The person on shore holds a long line that goes through an anchor. The line is attached to a float that has the dog's toy and a cadaver scent. Sometimes during water-search training, I used a pseudo-scent created in America; however, this artificial cadaver scent, which came in liquid form, was very expensive and nowhere near as good as the real thing. The gas emission from the carcass of a decomposed young pig is very similar to the scent of a dead human. But to use it in training, the carcass must be complete. The whole carcass should be placed in a plastic container punched with holes. The dog should then be allowed to play with the container. Later, the dog should be trained to indicate on it.

When a dog has completed most of its training, it will start to indicate in only a matter of minutes. Once that stage is mastered, the container should be hidden in the soil at various depths, and a long line should be attached to the dog's toy, which is buried above the cadaver. When the dog is over the spot, the toy should be pulled out of the ground by the person holding the line. This action confirms to the dog that this is a fun exercise, and will therefore increase the dog's drive to make the find. In training sessions, the dog should be encouraged to bark at the area where the container is buried, and also to dig and scratch the ground.

Over a period of weeks, training should be transferred to water. The dog should be taken out on a boat with a diver, who will pop up from the water every so often with the dog's toy. Later, the diver should introduce a cadaver scent and tease the dog with it. The diver should go under the water for a few seconds, pop up, then go back down again, repeating these actions several times to make sure to give the dog plenty of fun, which the dog quickly learns to associate with the cadaver scent.

Next, the training moves on to using a mobile anchor and

float. An anchor is placed in a river at least three feet deep. A line runs out from the anchor and back to the person on the shore. That person is critical to the training. Once the dog on the boat shows an interest or gives an indication, the person on shore releases the line and the float pops up out of the water with the dog's toy. The cadaver scent is also attached to the anchor and suspended about a foot under the water. But that never surfaces. The dog is then rewarded for responding. From then on, the line is extended further and further out until the dog can make a find located fifty feet under the water. If the dog can consistently find at the fifty-foot level over a series of twenty sessions, it's ready to go on a call-out accompanied by an experienced water-search dog. Once the experienced dog indicates, the inexperienced dog is brought in and observed to check if an indication is made on the same spot.

The biggest problem with search dogs is that humans simply don't know enough about them. Dogs are far more capable than we believe, and teaching a dog to detect cadaver scent is probably the easiest exercise in training a dog. Anyone can train any dog in this area. Cadaver training on land is the easiest of all; I could train a cadaver dog over a three or four-week period with just two or three sessions a day, each lasting just five minutes. It all comes back to the hunting instinct of dogs. Basically, it's a game of hide and seek. Even training a dog in drug detection is simple. Once a dog has a good hunting instinct, is a bit destructive and has drive, then it's only a matter of properly channelling that drive.

Anyone who has the time to walk a dog has the time to train that dog. Transferring the time from one exercise to the other is all it takes. One can imagine the difference that would make to our search resources in a time of crisis. If only people would change their way of thinking. Today, the need for dog handlers to train their dogs in water search is more pressing than ever as water-search call-outs are now much more frequent than mountain call-outs, mainly because the arrival of mobile phones has allowed people in trouble to call for help and explain where they are.

Bob became the first qualified water-search dog in the Republic of Ireland, and shortly after Holly and Zak finished their water-search training, the shout came to take part in one of the most distressing searches ever, when a spate of tragic events struck the banks of the River Slaney.

Sadness Along the Slaney

O f all the searches in which Áine was involved, the river search in Enniscorthy proved one of the most emotionally challenging. Over a six-day period beginning on 11 November 2002, four men went into the River Slaney from the Séamus Rafter Bridge in Enniscorthy, in separate incidents. Further downstream, a man entered the water at the village of Bunclody and another at Wexford. The six men ranged in age from nineteen to forty-one.

One of the men had entered the water on a weekday morning while children were on their way to school. Those children who saw the tragedy screamed with horror. When a lifebuoy was thrown in to save the man, he did not take it. Another man, a Latvian in his late twenties, was rescued. He had gone into the Slaney after he had failed to injure himself earlier by attempting to be run over by a car. The driver of the car and a local club doorman pulled him from the river. He was taken to Wexford General Hospital for treatment. The body of a nineteen-year-old apprentice carpenter from Bunclody was recovered ten hours after he entered the water. His best friend, from the same village, had taken his own life only three weeks earlier. The body of a twenty-eight-year-old man was also found. His family had already lost another young member when his sister was the victim of a car crash.

By 24 November two of the men who had entered the

Slaney at the Séamus Rafter Bridge in Enniscorthy and another who had entered the river at Wexford were still missing. One of the men was a thirty-four-year-old and the father of four children. An all-round sportsman, he had played Gaelic football and soccer, and had won a Leinster minor hurling medal in 1985. Another man, aged forty-one, was also still missing. He had worked as a barman for nineteen years in Enniscorthy. He left behind a wife and their two young children.

The search for the three remaining men was hampered by poor visibility and flooding, with the Slaney flowing rapidly at a speed of twelve miles per hour and threatening to burst its banks. Yet despite these dangerous conditions, huge numbers of volunteers continued to brave the flood-swollen waters in boats and canoes, with all search-and-rescue teams refusing to scale down their operations. Searchers included the Slaney Sea and Rescue Team, New Ross Search and Rescue, Mallow divers, the FCA, Civil Defence, mountain-rescue volunteers, and canoe and rowing clubs. On one day alone, more than seventy small vessels trawled up and down a fifteen-mile area, searching for the men's remains, determined to return them to their families, many of whom lined the riverbank, united in grief, staring hopelessly into the water, watching, waiting. Among them were the elderly parents of one of the missing men.

The people from Enniscorthy and the surrounding areas pooled together all their resources to help in the rescue operation. Many local employers gave their workers permission to stay away from work until the three remaining bodies had been recovered. Endless supplies of food poured in for the makeshift kitchen set up along the river bank to cater for the searchers. On average, 140 people were served snacks there daily. A fuel depot provided petrol free of charge. Local social and sporting events were cancelled. When the decision was taken to continue the search throughout Christmas Day if necessary, a local hotel offered to cook Christmas dinner for all the volunteers. The South Eastern Health Board set up a suicide help-line and provided a drop-in counselling centre in Enniscorthy. Seán McCarthy, a suicide resource officer with the health board, issued a warning to families to be on the lookout for copycat acts. The Samaritans sent in additional volunteers to the town. At the time, Harry O'Connor, chairman of the Slaney Sea and Rescue Team, lamented the scale of the tragedy: 'We've never had to deal with a tragedy like this. But then I don't think anybody in this country has.' Suicide statistics released that year showed that suicide rated as the second most common cause of death among young Irish males.

The shout came. Áine set out for Midleton at six o'clock in the morning to meet up with Noel Murphy and his dog Holly. Áine had only recently learned to drive, and she was banking on Noel to take over at the wheel. When she arrived at Noel's house, the place was in darkness. All the curtains were closed. She rang the doorbell and phoned repeatedly, but got no reply. Eventually, Noel appeared. 'I've only just got to bed, two hours' sleep. You'll have to drive.'

At that point, Áine was still fairly new to real-life searches. In her eyes, Holly was a funny-looking dog, with her strange, triangular-shaped head. But she knew, like the rest of us, that Holly was good, really good, with a history to prove it. Holly had already taken part in seven other search operations, all of which were water searches, but nobody had ever been recovered alive.

They arrived in Enniscorthy and went straight to a briefing, which was held in a large lorry container parked on the banks of the Slaney. Volunteers – among them Harry O'Connor's wife – were inside, helping to prepare and dish up food. Family members of the missing men were also there. They were busy serving soup and sandwiches, filling mugs of tea and coffee, fussing over everyone else as if they themselves needed no attention or consideration. Áine's heart was breaking at the sight of them. She couldn't help but think of those poor unfortunate men and how, if they could see this now, they'd realise the extent of the pain.

Shane O'Connor, the son of Harry O'Connor, had been on duty one night for two hours. Shane rang his father in a worried state to say that there was a girl on the banks of the river talking on her mobile phone and crying. Harry asked Shane if he had anyone else with him. Shane said that Dario Anetta, the volunteer who was supposed to be on watch with him, had not turned up. Unknown to Shane, Dario was actually on duty only two hundred yards up the quay, unaware that Shane was nearby. He had also spotted the sobbing girl and was keeping a close eye on her. Before the father and son had finished their conversation, the girl had jumped into the river. Dario and Shane both quickly followed, and saved her.

Áine, Noel and Holly were taken to the banks of the

Slaney, which were a hundred yards wide on either side of the river and now heavily flooded – so much so that it was necessary to call off the twenty-four-hour watch on the river even though it was not only to keep a lookout for the missing bodies but also to prevent any further drownings. However, the volunteers' own safety had to be considered as well, and allowing them to work there in those conditions was too dangerous.

Now Holly could take over. With Áine and Noel, she combed all along the banks, up and down at either side, undeterred by the wet, boggy ground. Áine and Noel reported back to Harry O'Connor, and assured him that Holly had found nothing along the way. Then they were taken out in a boat with Holly, away from the town. The river was deep and flowing fast. Keeping a close eye on Holly was important. If she gave any indication, the driver would have to be signalled immediately. He would need to turn the boat around, and then move over the exact spot again to get a confirmation of the indication.

The morning was extremely cold, and Áine and Noel took it in turns to hold Holly as their hands were growing numb. Every now and then along the way, they were hit by low branches. The riverside was thick with reeds that slowed the pace and made the search more difficult. Not far from the town – beside the main Enniscorthy to Wexford road – there came into view a massive, red-brick, flat-roofed building, with barred-up windows and a rectangular tower on top – almost like a watch tower. It was situated on high ground, peering down over the river, the town and its people, keeping them in view, reminding them of its existence, a symbol of power. The driver said it was St Senan's – Enniscorthy's psychiatric hospital. Áine felt the shivers run up her spine.

All along the river, Holly remained fully focused. She gave a few indications by barking. They noted the exact location, moved on down the river, and came back again to double-check. They combed constantly up and down the water, at both sides. At one stage, when the driver went into reverse, they were almost thrown overboard – a reminder that searchers put their own lives at risk while they work.

Having taken a short lunch break, they worked right through the afternoon, eventually calling it a day, satisfied with Holly's consistent indications that would allow the divers to concentrate their search.

The search for the remaining three men lasted almost six weeks, until all bodies were recovered. The last three bodies were all located within a 500-yard stretch from where Holly had indicated. The body of the man who entered the river in Wexford was found on Rosslare Strand after twenty days, while the remains of the first man to enter the water on 11 November became the last body to be recovered, on 20 December.

The memories of the search haunted Áine for some time to come. The suffering of the families, the iciness of the river, and the torment hanging over Enniscorthy kept playing on her mind. Recently, the mental-health commission visited St Senan's and recommended that the old red-brick building should be closed down and that alternative care should be provided in the community for long-term patients.

Today, the makeshift kitchen set up in the truck container in 2002 still stands in the same spot on the banks of the Slaney – a poignant reminder of one dreadful, bleak, cold, wet November when the people from the town of Enniscorthy and surrounding areas came together as one, united in their grief for the men who perished in the river.

Ninety-one and Missing

A ninety-one-year-old man disappeared on Friday 20 June 2003, having attended a local football match. He was last seen at Moanroe Cross, Clonmel. There was no obvious explanation for his disappearance, but neighbours believed that the elderly, widowed father of four might have set out to visit a friend that night on his way back to his farm at Caherclough, Lisronagh, near Clonmel. From the outset, there was great worry for his safety, not only because of his age but also because he suffered from Alzheimer's disease.

The gardaí issued repeated appeals for information and for help from the public, describing the missing farmer as being of medium height and build, wearing glasses, walking with a slight stoop and using a walking stick. When no clues to his whereabouts came to light, a major search-and-rescue operation got underway. This involved the South East Mountain Rescue Team, SARDA, the Garda Air Support Team, Civil Defence, Air Corps and hundreds of volunteers, including local farmers who abandoned saving crops in their fields to search for the missing man.

Once I heard about the case, I phoned the gardaí and offered the services of our search dogs. The search co-ordinators involved said they already had plenty of dogs and people out searching. Among those dogs was Eiger, my second-certified, upgraded search dog, who was on loan to SARDA and was now being handled by a woman from Clonmel who was a very experienced dog handler and had, over the years, a number of dogs in training but had not certified any as a search dog. Eventually, despite her many years of experience in dog handling, she had to be certified as a search-dog handler, which meant taking part with Eiger in an assessment, which she passed.

During the week, I made two more phone calls and repeated the offer of help. Finally, at around 4 p.m. on the Wednesday – the fifth day of the search – I got the shout. Straight away, I contacted the other members of our dog team, and three car loads of us set off in convoy for Caherclough. Our team included Áine, Noel Murphy and Richard Cotter. Noel took seven-year-old Holly, and I had Bob. Both dogs were trained to search for live bodies and cadavers. Such cross-training can be easily achieved, although most other countries consider it complicated, and consequently tend to specialise in only one area or the other. On average, in nine out of ten searches, only one person is found alive. If anything, the figures justify the necessity for cross-training all dogs.

When we reached Caherclough at about 7.30 p.m., all of the other searchers were leaving to go home. As we made our way into the search area, some of the SARDA dog handlers passed us on the way out, with Eiger in tow. When our briefing was finished, three fields were pointed out to us as our search areas. These particular fields were only third or fourth on the list of probable areas, which is always drawn up prior to the commencement of a search operation and based mainly on likely chosen directions, taking into consideration the missing person's profile.

Around the edges of these fields, there were many drainage channels about five feet deep and five feet square. These drains were dangerous as, being covered by brambles and trees, they were invisible. Noel and I, being the two dog handlers on site, took a field each. Our strategy was to search the perimeters first. This was a natural choice as it would be an obvious area for anyone seeking shelter – even animals make for the borders in bad weather. The perimeter of a field should always be checked at the outset as it's there that a dog is likely to pick up any scent present in the field.

After only forty-five minutes, Noel contacted me on the radio to say he had found the missing man in the fourteen-acre cornfield. He was lying on his back in a furrow created by a tractor wheel in the perimeter, about five feet from the ditch, and was shielded by overhanging trees. As that particular area was not sown with corn, he was visible. These fields were more than familiar to him: he would have walked them regularly on his way to the river to fish.

At first, it was thought that the man was not alive. However, as I approached him, I could see the rise and fall of his chest. Áine arrived and immediately took the man's head in her lap and began to speak with him. He gripped Áine's hand very tightly and repeatedly pleaded with her not to leave him. Áine told him how we had been searching 'for hours' and were not going to leave him now. He was severely dehydrated, sunburnt and very weak. He was wearing a heavy, tweed overcoat over lots of other warm clothing. He continued to grip Áine's hand so tightly that it began to hurt, but she didn't mind because it showed that he still had some strength left in him after his terrible ordeal.

Áine was on a high, thrilled to bits that the missing man had been found alive. This was by far the best part of search and rescue: sensing that you can make a difference by training the dogs, and that you can save people's lives even though all the odds might seem stacked against you. She was now more committed than ever to a future as a search-dog handler.

Shortly afterwards, the man said he would love some porridge and a toasted sausage sandwich. Then he asked the name of the dog responsible for finding him. Apparently, he had become disorientated as he walked up the long avenue to his cottage. He had gone off the path and taken the easiest route, which was downhill, until eventually he could go no further.

Noel phoned the gardaí to tell them the missing man had been found alive. They would not believe him, and thought it was a joke. It took a second phone call from Áine before they were convinced. A half-hour later, all hell broke loose. Jeeps and ambulances appeared from nowhere. The man's delighted family arrived, with elation and relief written all over their faces.

At the debriefing, we heard that the field where the man was found had been searched a few times in the previous days. One of the rescue helicopters had a heat-seeking device that projects a beam beneath its flight path and reflects the source of the heat. The helicopter had flown over the cornfield, but the pilot explained that the high trees over the furrows had probably obstructed the detection of any heat there, and also prevented any sighting of the missing man from the air. One of the gardaí added that the man's body could have been so cold that heat detection may have been impossible. Both explanations were legitimate.

The field must have been searched on foot by inexperienced searchers. If the field had been searched in a co-ordinated manner, they would undoubtedly have found the elderly man. Even if one civilian searcher had walked the perimeter, that person would have had to trip over the missing man to get by. Some of the searchers at the debriefing would not accept that the missing man had been lying in the same spot for five nights and five days. They insisted that they had walked that cornfield many times and that he must have wandered in there only that day. They would not accept that they had missed him.

He was found only eight hundred yards from where he was last seen, and there is no doubt in our minds that, in this particular case, a bloodhound, if called in early, would have found him in a very short time. When scent leaves a body, the wind spreads it in a variety of ways and forms a rough cone. Once an experienced search dog enters the scent cone, he will strike, usually alerting the handler by putting up his tail and head, and sniffing.

The man was taken to St Joseph's Hospital in Clonmel, where he made a good recovery. As he was both a fisherman and hunter, he was well used to the outdoors all his life. For his age, he was a hardy man, and his resilience had definitely stood to him. The fact that the weather had been mild throughout his ordeal had also helped him to survive.

Holly was hailed as the heroine of the night. She was rewarded for finding the missing man by having a ball thrown over and back to her. All she wanted was a game of catch. With the media focus on Red Cross Search Dogs, we used it wisely by appealing to people to get involved in the volunteer rescue service, and to train their dogs for search-and-rescue work. There is no reason whatsoever why every town in Ireland should not have such a search-and-rescue dog service, especially as training a dog to be a search dog takes only the same amount of time each day as it does to walk a dog, and any dog that hunts is capable of being trained to be a search dog. Specially trained dogs could be called in early and used before large-scale searches begin and hundreds of searchers start trekking across lands and ruining the scent left by the missing person. In Ireland, in addition to the Garda Dog Unit, there are just a few volunteer search-and-rescue dogs, whereas in other countries it's a statutory requirement to provide such a service locally.

A week or two after finding the missing man, Áine returned to visit him. She found him in great spirits. Noel, an ambulance driver, regularly called to see him, as on occasion he transferred patients in and out of the hospital where the man was happily being tended to by the nurses and staff in St Joseph's.

Sadly, when Áine and I went back again only six months later, we were making the journey to attend his funeral, following his death from natural causes.

Understanding Lucy

One Sunday in the summer of 2003, a woman's bicycle was found abandoned at the bottom of a hill outside the village of Newcastle West, County Limerick. As part of the woman's normal Sunday-morning routine, she always left her bike there, in exactly the same spot, and then walked the remaining mile to the village. But on this occasion, she never returned to collect the bike, and disappeared without a trace. Locals said she was physically fit but thought that she might have become disorientated.

Áine, Noel Murphy and Richard Cotter joined the search at 11 p.m. that day, along with Zak, Bob and Holly. The area surrounding the bicycle was so vast that it was almost impossible to decide where to start or which sections to prioritise. Áine and Zak began their search three fields away from the bike. In one of the fields they searched, the ferns had grown to at least six feet in height, making it nearly impossible for anyone to walk through. Áine had to crawl to make progress. They combed through their allocated area for seven hours but found no clues as to the direction the missing woman may have taken. Noel, Richard and their dogs were also out of luck.

At 6 a.m. Áine – exhausted and drained – threw herself down on the grass at the top of a hilly field. Zak lay down beside her. She felt burnt-out, defeated and crushed. Surely there was a better, easier, quicker way to break down areas when searching for a missing person? The whole search-dog scenario was getting to her. She felt annoyed that in most searches the dogs were not called in early enough, which made their work more difficult and lessened their chances of success. Air-scenting dogs had to work extremely hard because scent lingers everywhere. Their work rate was phenomenal.

She sat thinking, gazing hopelessly towards the sky; the low-hanging clouds matched her sullen mood. Then, as she watched, still deep in thought, a magnificent sunrise began to break through, leaving the bleak of night behind, brightening the landscape all around, bringing hope of a new day, the promise of a fresh start. Her mind suddenly turned to bloodhounds – for years known as 'racist dogs' because they were used in the US to track down slaves and by whites in Africa to catch poachers. People wrongly perceive bloodhounds as intimidating, when they are, in fact, merely hunters. Áine pondered the possibility of using bloodhounds here in Ireland, weighing up what they had to offer in comparison to air-scenting dogs. As air-scenting dogs look for human scent as opposed to a specific scent, they often have to spend much time eliminating others from the search, depending on how many people are present. If the missing person is at the top of a mountain and an air-scenting dog starts at the bottom, the dog may have to search the entire mountain before making the find. Precious time is lost. If bloodhounds are used, they can take the scent from where the missing person was last seen and trail directly to that person, saving much time and effort as they concentrate on a specific scent. The more Áine thought about it, the more convinced she became that bloodhounds would have a higher rate of success in search operations than air-scenting dogs. Bloodhounds, she decided, were the way forward, the better option.

The missing woman turned up safe and well, without the aid of searchers. She simply walked unannounced into a neighbour's house. The locals were right: she had become temporarily confused, lost her way and wandered, thinking she was going somewhere else.

But the failed search in Newcastle West proved a turning point for Áine and, indeed, for all of us, as she returned home filled with a fire and determination that no earthly power could quench. Her mind was set on owning a bloodhound. But nobody believed she would actually make the move, least of all me.

Once Áine got her hands on a list of hunting packs, there was no stopping her. She contacted Nick Wheeler, an East Sussex breeder, and begged him to put her name on his list for a pup. Breeders are slow to give up their lines easily; they want genuine owners who are not in it for the money. Nick wasn't willing to commit straight away, but Áine annoyed the hell out of him until she finally got what she wanted.

Lucy was flown over from Heathrow to Cork airport at the age of just twelve weeks. She had gone from a hunting kennels to a plane, and must have been terrified. On her crate was written 'Hi, I'm Farcry Delphinium! Please talk to me.' Farcry was actually the name of the kennels from which she had come, and delphinium, the flower, was simply added on. As the guy at Cork airport handed over the crate to Áine, he said, 'What a stupid bloody name to give a dog!'

Áine drove up to me at work, proud as punch with the pup in the back. The poor dog looked scared out of her mind! She had big, long ears, almost black. But her colour lightened as she got older. I couldn't believe Áine had actually done it! She began training her straight away. Soon, Lucy was swaggering around the place full of herself, as if to say 'I'm miles too good for here!' And she *was* good, and quickly showed what she was made of by making her first find at only ten months. In a way Lucy was a guinea pig, as she was the first bloodhound to be trained in Ireland for work as a search-and-rescue dog. From the very beginning, she had a great drive to work. She was a natural hunting dog and had a good instinct. Trying to exercise her like a normal dog was almost impossible as she'd drop her head and track anyone who had walked the path before her.

Her English breeders, Sue and Nick Wheeler, kept in constant contact by phone. They checked up on her progress and gave advice. But it took me a good twelve months before I could make any sense of how a bloodhound worked. Before I tried my hand at training Lucy, Áine had already put in a good deal of work with her. Having been an active member of K-9, Áine already had plenty of doggy experience behind her. She had been involved in many notable rescues throughout Ireland with her air-scenting dog Zak, an active water-search dog with nine confirmed finds to his credit. She had also trained in *schutzhund*, and fully understood tracking dogs. Now she was committed to learning all she could about trailing dogs and to giving Lucy the best possible training. From what I could see, she was making a great job of it.

When I decided to get involved, I had to start from scratch. I knew absolutely nothing about bloodhounds. I came from a different tradition of dogs that had taught me all about tracking dogs and air-scenting dogs – so much so that I was dubious about bloodhounds. I was entering totally new territory and stepping way outside my comfort zone. I began the training session by putting Lucy on a long, thirty-foot lead. I sent a body walking ahead, down one particular side of the road. When we set off, Lucy veered to the opposite side. But she was obviously picking up scent there as the wind can carry off scent in all directions. Even a passing car can whisk it away and sprinkle it over other areas. The scent might rest along by ditches or settle down on bushes or briars. Lucy never worked in a straight line. She trawled along, over and back. She forged ahead with speed. I held onto the lead with all my might as she dragged me along behind her with force, almost pulling the hands off me as I tried to keep up. If she lost a scent, she backtracked without hesitation. Then she circled wide until she picked it up again.

The body laid markers for me along the way to show the direction taken. When training, it's essential that the dog always makes a successful find. Markers – such as toilet paper or flags – are used to mark turns and directions of the trail-layer. Should a young dog totally lose the trail, the handler can guide the bloodhound back onto the right path. It also gives the handler confidence in the dog when the dog makes the correct turns. A piece of white paper under a tree meant that the body had turned right. A pink piece signalled a left turn. A stick in the ground indicated another turning point. Sometimes, the body entered a field, walked on for twenty yards, then backtracked for another fifty yards and took a different course. But I never knew exactly where the body was hiding. I relied on the markers to guide me while carefully reading Lucy's body language and watching how she behaved at every turning point. Sometimes, I asked the person laying the trail to park a car at the bottom of a mountain to allow Lucy to take scent from it and to begin her search from there. Other times, I laid a track from one point to another, usually starting at the Bishopstown end on the outskirts of Cork city. The body would stand at a door of Dunnes Stores in Bishopstown, walk out a few miles beyond the viaduct, and mark the exact finishing point. A few days later, the body would drive to that marker, park the car there, and wait. I would then give Lucy a scented article, and leave her to track from the door of Dunnes Stores out to where the body was hiding in a spot close to the car.

Lucy was only ten months old when she became involved in her first ever real-life water search. At the time, she was far from being fully trained, and at least a year away from qualifying as a mission-ready dog. But the gardaí decided to try her, along with Noel Murphy's dog Holly, as we had no other search dogs available on the night. Richard Cotter also came on board, and headed for east Cork with Áine, Noel and the dogs. The missing elderly man was last seen around midnight several nights before as he left a pub in the village of Castlelyons. Searchers – including other dog units and three different diving teams – had already trawled through the surrounding fields and nearby river but had found nothing.

Water holds scents better than land. It has a magnetic pull. As a flow of air always follows the current, scent can become distorted, and this can cause it to lodge underneath river banks, on grass or weeds. A pillowcase from the missing man's bedroom was produced as a scent article. As the dogs began their search, Lucy tracked the scent from the pub and trailed swiftly downhill through the village until she came to Bride's Bridge. She overshot the gate on the bridge. Then she seemed to lose the scent and doubled back. She went through an iron gate – an opening in the wall of an old manor house – then crossed over to the edge of the river bank and immediately began to give tongue, which is one of the vocal sounds a bloodhound makes. She became excited and tried to jump into the river. Áine had a long line on Lucy, and happened to look back up at the bridge. At that very moment, she saw a little old man standing on the bridge. He took off his hat, blessed himself, and walked away, almost as if he fully trusted the dog's instinct. Áine suggested they concentrate their efforts on the river. Within only a matter of hours, they found the body of the missing man in the water.

Lucy also indicated correctly at Doneraile Park during a search for a missing man. She gave a strong indication in a stream leading to a lake, despite the protestations of a sub-aqua volunteer group that there was no way there was a body in the water. Áine was adamant. Her hands were blistered from trying to hold Lucy, and her knees were bruised from Lucy dragging her through the stream that connected up with the lake. Weeks later, while a girl was boating on the lake – which was crystal clear that day – she saw the body of the missing man in the lake.

At a very young age, Lucy had proved her worth as a search-and-rescue dog. Now she was about to play a part in one of the most high-profile searches ever to take place in Ireland: the search for a young boy from Midleton, County Cork.

The Missing Schoolboy

The town of Midleton in east Cork changed forever on 4 January 2005 when a young boy was reported missing. A massive search got underway, and only hours later Noel Murphy rang me. He happened to be a friend of the boy's family. His message was brief: 'Be on standby.' He reminded me that I had met the lad once, when Noel had brought him along with his own son – the two boys were pals – to one of our training days in The Vee.

Around midnight, the shout came. Áine and I drove to Midleton with our air-scenting dogs, Zak and Bob. We headed for the golf club, where the gardaí had set up the base for the search, and we signed in with the garda controller at his desk in a corner of the lounge. Then we listened to a briefing, which covered details about the eleven-year-old schoolboy, such as a description of his clothing, the fact that he was afraid of the dark, and that he suffered from ADHD (attention deficit hyperactivity disorder). When it came to selecting local guides for us, the missing boy's next-door neighbour and friend, a twenty-year-old engineering student, was asked by the gardaí to accompany Áine. His brother was teamed up with me. Áine was given the golf course and river as her search areas. I was asked to search the Ballyedmond countryside around the missing child's home.

Beginning our search around 1 a.m. suited us as air-scenting dogs work best in the dark and most of the other searchers had already gone home, which eliminated their scent from the scene. Our starting point with Bob focused on areas close to the boy's house, which was situated in a row of large houses. The family home of the two brothers who were our guides was next door. A laneway separated the two houses, which were about sixty yards apart.

In the quiet black of night, we combed through play areas used by the eleven-year-old and other local children, including a tree house built for the child by Áine's guide, the twenty-year-old student. We examined outbuildings and farmlands. We scoured our way through ditches, fields and woodlands. As we searched on through the early hours, I kept calling the boy's name aloud. We always work under the assumption that the missing person is lying injured somewhere. Even if missing persons can't answer back, they become reassured that at least someone is out looking for them. My guide kept on calling the child's name, too. Other than that, he said very little. Even when we stopped to rest, he rarely spoke.

According to Áine, his brother was the total opposite. He chatted non-stop, and told Áine that the boy had come off his medication for ADHD. When Áine said, 'You were the last person to see him alive,' he answered, 'Yeah.' He seemed to become jittery and upset then, but Áine took no notice as her focus was on finding the missing boy. When they rested, he showed great interest in how the dogs worked. He asked about a tracking dog's ability, and wanted to know if the scent of a missing person could be detected in a car or in a river.

Although Áine had constantly called out the child's name, her guide never joined in.

At around 5 a.m. Áine fell and twisted her ankle. At that stage, our two search teams were about half a mile apart. As Áine could do no more, she headed back to the van with Zak, while her guide contacted his brother to find out our whereabouts. He joined up with us while we were searching a farmyard, and stayed with us for the rest of the search. Any time we stopped, he chatted and asked questions about the dogs. He seemed especially interested in the possible use of bloodhounds, and his questions were questions that any person with a genuine interest in dogs and the search would ask. He told me that the missing boy was highly strung, and said he had probably fallen into the river.

He had a theory about the child's missing bicycle. There had been no sign of his new, silver BMX, which he had left outside his next-door neighbour's house. Then, after word spread that he was missing, a father and son notified the gardaí that they had found the bike earlier that evening, lying against a ditch at the side of the road several hundred yards from the missing child's house in the direction of the golf course. However, the student told me that he believed the bike had probably not been left there by the missing boy, and that it had more than likely been stolen from outside the student's gate, where the child had parked it. He was convinced that when news spread that the boy was missing, panic set in and the bike was returned.

To me, the student seemed a very nice, pleasant guy, and he appeared calm and cool. Nothing about him suggested that he could possibly have anything to do with the disappearance of the young boy. He had been searching with us for about two hours when his mother phoned him to ask how he and his brother were doing and to find out their location. At this stage, we were only a few minutes' walk from their house. All three of us were wet and tired. I decided we should call it a day as we needed a rest and other searchers would be arriving soon. We walked together to the brothers' gate, and the two young men went in home.

Before I headed away for a few hours' sleep, I reported back to the gardaí at base on how the search had gone. I told them about the student's theory regarding the bike, but they did not comment as they never say anything to hamper any future investigations. When we got home, Áine kept saying that there was something strange about her guide. I thought she was tired, and told her to get some sleep.

Around midday Áine and I returned to Midleton as the controller had asked us to continue with the search. At the base, we joined the queues of people waiting to be told where to go, and to get a briefing. In some cases, especially where teams were involved, team leaders were selected and a general briefing was given to them by one of the gardaí. In such a search, where the number of searchers reached well over a thousand, briefing everyone individually was out of the question.

Áine was now accompanied by her young bloodhound Lucy. While air-scenting dogs are trained to sniff out any human smell, Lucy was trained to search for one specific scent. Usually, the strongest scents of all can be found in a person's bedroom. To avoid contamination, the item chosen for scenting purposes must be taken up with a pair of tongs, placed in a sealed plastic bag, and then put into a second sealed container. Lucy took the missing schoolboy's scent from a pillowcase belonging to him. When Lucy was taken to the spot where the child's bike had allegedly been left, she failed to pick up his scent. The student's theory about the bike seemed to add up. On the other hand, the bike might actually have been found there as, earlier, grass and briars had been cut away from the ditch in an effort to find clues, and the scent could thereby have been ruined. A question mark hung over it.

Working without a guide, Áine continued with Lucy further along the golf-course road. At a sharp bend on the road, they came to the gate of a field, which Áine wanted to enter. When she couldn't open the gate, she noticed several youngsters a few yards away, the student among them. Áine asked him to open the gate, and was amazed when he paid no attention to her, especially as they had worked together only hours before. Eventually, he came over and opened it. Once they were inside the field, Lucy body-banged him; she jumped right up on him. Áine still didn't suspect a thing, but she should have. We had been training Lucy to compete in bloodhound trials in the UK, and this required that the dog, on completion of the trial, should acknowledge the trail-layers by picking them out from within a group of people and identifying them by jumping on them. Lucy howled all the way down the field, which led as the crow flies to East Cork Oil, with the river close by. Still nothing clicked with Áine. A

Coast Guard helicopter was flying overhead, and there were loads of other searchers in the area, but Lucy wasn't bothered – she got on with the search.

When I met up with Áine later, she said, 'I'm so ashamed of Lucy. She jumped up on top of the guide I was with last night.' I thought nothing of it either. We should have been more alert, but we were so focused on finding the missing child that we simply never stopped to look at the bigger picture. The fact that Lucy was a young bloodhound also entered into it, as at that point we hadn't been working with her long enough to trust her fully. But something kept niggling at Áine, and when she signed out at the search base later that day, she mentioned to one of the older gardaí that she thought there was something strange about the student. The garda nodded but said nothing. Áine added that Lucy had jumped up on him, but felt she was being ignored and so she walked away.

That particular day, Bob and I were accompanied by a garda. The controller had asked us to concentrate on certain fields, a massive area of over a hundred acres. It was a nightmare. The worst thing you can have in any search is a load of unsupervised civilians. Everywhere we went, there were at least five other groups of independent searchers, each group consisting of four or five people. Most of them were unsupervised, volunteer searchers, and many of them walked around aimlessly. Some had not even bothered to sign in, yet signing in and out is essential, not only to get instructions on where to search but also to let the controller keep track of all searchers, note areas covered, and ensure that everyone returns safely to base. While these volunteers were well-meaning people, they were ruining the trained dog searchers' chances of finding the missing child, and were creating the possibility of unknowingly interfering with evidence.

The following day, Bob and I searched Curragh Woods, which lies in a long, narrow glen, with a river flowing alongside. Other trained searchers there were frustrated by the number of unsupervised volunteers in the area, who were proving more of a hindrance than a help. It was obvious that the concentration levels of these independent searchers were low. They were chatting non-stop. Concentration in a search is never easy. A searcher is probably effective for only about an hour or two at a time. Having constantly looked at the ground for clues that may lead to a body, tiredness sets in and the eyes give up.

As the days and nights went by, the fear among local parents for their own children kept growing – more so when it came to light that there were some registered paedophiles in the area. According to the newspapers, locals only became aware of their presence when the paedophiles were brought in for questioning by the gardaí.

Having spent several days searching, I had to go back to work. By then, a young German woman called Jenny, who had trained with us for twelve months, had joined the search with her two dogs, a Briard-collie-cross and a collie-shepherd named Noah and Peramus. Both had been certified by the German police as search dogs, and she searched with the dogs for five or six days but was unsuccessful.

On Wednesday 12 January everyone's worst fears were realised. The boy's mobile phone had been traced to an isolated area near Inch Strand, about eleven miles from Midleton. Even when a mobile phone is switched off, it gives off a faint signal. Two men – searching as part of a group of volunteers led by army and garda personnel – were combing through the area, when they came upon a small body hidden in gorse and scrub at the side of a bóthairín leading to the beach. The body was partly covered in plastic and appeared to have been dumped. Later, the fingerprints taken from the plastic sheeting proved vital. Back at base, news that a body had been found came out over an open microphone in a room full of journalists. Shortly afterwards, the remains were identified as the body of the missing child. A post-mortem showed he had died of asphyxiation.

On the day of the boy's funeral, the town of Midleton came to a standstill. The funeral Mass at the Church of the Most Holy Rosary can only be described as extremely sad and distressing. For the first time, Áine and I saw the child's heartbroken parents. Often, when searchers meet the families of the missing while a search is ongoing, the searchers' commitment intensifies and they find it hard to give up the search without finding the missing person. They become hooked. In the churchyard afterwards, people huddled together in groups, talking and consoling each other, overcome with grief, genuinely heartbroken. Many of them were searchers who had come to pay their respects.

Already, the rumour mill was spinning out of control. People whispered that the gardaí had over thirty suspects on their list. But nobody was prepared for what was around the corner, as another local family was about to become part of the terrible tragedy. Within days of the boy's funeral, news broke that an arrest had been made. The man taken into custody and charged with the manslaughter of the young boy was shown on TV3 news. Although his face was not visible, Áine immediately recognised him as the student who had acted as her guide and whom Lucy had body-banged. 'I knew it!' she said. 'I knew the dog was right!' She was fuming to think that he had gone out searching with her through the night instead of going down to the garda barracks to make a confession. She felt even worse about having failed to pick up on what Lucy had been trying to tell her. I was dumbfounded. I just couldn't get my head around it. Never in a million years would I have thought he could possibly be responsible. The words Neil Powell had tried to drill into us over and over again at training sessions in the Wicklow and Mourne Mountains came ringing in my ears: 'Always trust your dog.'

People on the street were traumatised by the arrest, with the sympathies and loyalties of many now becoming torn between the two neighbouring families at the centre of the tragedy.

Áine and I were called to the garda barracks to make a statement about how we became involved in the search, how we carried out our search, what the student said on the night, and if there was anything that stood out about the case. Later, we were summoned to the Central Criminal Court sitting in Cork. The atmosphere there was very official. We were asked if the student had shown an interest in a tracking dog's ability to detect scent in a car or in a river, and in the use of bloodhounds. We got little chance to say much else, and felt we had failed to give Lucy the credit she deserved. After the hearing, we stood at the back of the court, and when the state solicitor came along, we told him how disillusioned we were with the whole procedure, which had denied us the chance to give our full story. 'Sometimes, all you can do is give yes or no answers,' he said. 'That's just the way the system is.'

The student was sentenced to four years in prison for the manslaughter of the young boy. He was released on 16 January 2008, having served three years.

Drownings at Owenahincha

It was the first Sunday in September 2006. Owenahincha beach in west Cork was a little quieter than usual as the summer season was drawing to a close, the schools had reopened, and most of the families who had summer houses or mobile homes in the area had returned home. But there was still plenty of activity, with children playing in the sand and strollers on the beach striding along at their ease. Among them was a twenty-three-year-old undergraduate, who was leisurely walking along with his parents, enjoying their company and having a chat. The young man had much to look forward to in life. He was a gifted soccer player who had played in the Collingwood Cup, and was due to graduate from UCC in only a matter of weeks. When a young couple in the water started screaming for help, the young man threw off his shoes and ran into the sea to save the drowning pair, as his mother, fearing for his safety, pleaded with him not to go.

At the same time, another young man – a thirty-seven-year-old businessman – was walking the strand with his fiancée. They happened to be in the area having attended a wedding in nearby Rosscarbery the day before. Their own wedding was planned for the following February. Once the young man saw the couple struggling in the sea, he grabbed the nearest lifebuoy and raced as fast as he could into the water.

On that Sunday morning, conditions on the strand were bright and breezy. But the ocean was wild and treacherous. During the week, tides had been extremely high, and, as a result, the currents and undertow were much more powerful than usual. There were no lifeguards on duty; lifeguards had been employed at the beach all through the summer months by Cork County Council, and their contracts had expired only two days before.

As the drowning pair grabbed the lifebuoy from their rescuers and clutched it with all their might, a huge wave enveloped them, swept them crossways in the direction of the strand, and brought them safely back to shore. The two young men who had jumped in to save them were left behind to struggle in the angry sea. Both men were good swimmers, but they were no match for the swelling waters at Owenahincha, which quickly overpowered them and carried them further out to sea. By the time help arrived minutes later, both men had disappeared from sight. On shore, an ambulance crew treated the surviving couple for shock and hypothermia. Both had come to Owenahincha for a local market; she was from Kilkenny, and he was originally from Wales and had been living near Bantry for the past year.

The following Tuesday, the body of the thirty-seven-year-old rescuer was found in deep waters directly off Owenahincha by *Gaia*, a trawler based in Union Hall, west Cork. There was no trace of the remains of the younger man.

Days later, the missing man's mother contacted my sister Celine, and asked if I would be willing to join in the search for her son. Celine knew him well as he had worked with her part-time while at college. Without delay, Celine, Áine, Glen and I drove to Owenahincha. Áine took along Zak, and I brought Bob. Glen volunteered to act as liaison. We met the controller of the search, Brian Lotty, a teacher from Riverstown and a friend of the missing man's family. In the field of search and rescue, Brian was an amateur and had never before taken on such a task but did so at the personal request of the family. But he was some operator: of all the controllers I've ever seen in action – and the vast majority of them would have been professional – he was by far the best. He was efficient, straight-talking and had an air of authority about him. Everything was organised down to the last detail: fuel tankers for the boats, food for the searchers, nothing was overlooked – he was the ideal controller.

Having listened to his excellent briefing, Áine, Celine and Zak stayed on shore to carry out a land search. Bob and I went out on the sea with a diving team in an RIB (rigid inflatable boat). From the shoreline, the sea was deceiving. It looked calm and smooth. But the swell of the ocean was actually huge.

In water searches, intense concentration is necessary. You can't afford to be distracted or to take your eyes off the water as the missing person may pop up for only a second before becoming totally submerged again. Staring continuously down into the water and the moving current becomes tiring. If the watch lasts for more than a few hours, you are likely to become ineffective due to exhaustion. At best, my concentration levels would probably be effective for two to three hours, no more.

Only twenty minutes into the search, when we were only a mile or two from shore, Bob gave his first indication. He began to whine like a child, which is his natural way of signalling the scent of a dead body, just like Eiger. Both of them were always very sensitive dogs. One of the other three men on board noted Bob's indication on a map, as well as the distance from the shoreline and a rock within our view.

We moved on along the shore, then swung around and came back. We wanted to check if Bob would repeat the indication at the same point. Sure enough, he indicated again on almost the identical spot. Knowing how Bob behaved, I told the crew that if we stayed any longer at the point of indication, Bob would become so frustrated that he was likely to jump off the boat. On making a find, a dog expects his favourite toy to pop out of the water, as that is how we train them, and Bob was now growing impatient. We moved on once again.

All day long, the garda and navy divers had been out searching in the waters. As they were fairly near us – maybe only a quarter of a mile away – we made contact with them on the radio to fill them in on Bob's indication. They moved up alongside us in their RIBs. To show them what was happening, we circled around again and then returned to the scent cone. As I wanted everyone to see that I was not influencing Bob's behaviour, I turned my back to him. Seconds later, one of the divers shouted at me that Bob was trying to jump into the sea. I was in no doubt that Bob was getting scent from the water, but I was also aware that the current and winds can influence the point from where the scent rises. The divers noted the area of indication. They then decided to call a halt for the day as it was becoming too late to continue diving. They suggested they would begin from the same spot the following morning, and work towards the shoreline. We all headed back to base, where Brian Lotty gave an excellent debriefing.

Meanwhile, on shore, Zak had also given an indication. He had been standing with Áine and Celine on a rock – known locally as Submarine Rock – when he signalled. The area he barked at was located somewhere between the shoreline and our RIB. His indication matched Bob's.

On the Saturday, I returned to the scene at around 10 a.m. as the controller had phoned to ask us to continue the search. I was taken out on the sea with Bob on another RIB. The other searchers, who had started earlier that morning, had intensified their search of the area surrounding the point of indication given by Zak and Bob. We hadn't been out very long in the water when we got a phone call to say that they had found the body of the young man. It had been washed up near Submarine Rock, the place where Zak had indicated. Later, the navy gave credit to Bob and Zak by saying that the body had been located because everyone had concentrated on the area indicated by the dogs. They were so impressed with how the dogs had worked that they very generously invited us along with the dogs to train at their water facility at the naval base.

Áine and I couldn't bring ourselves to attend the young man's removal. At the time, it seemed the right thing to do – maybe we were just too close to the tragedy and knew too much about him and his family because of the links with Celine. As searchers, we often try to ignore the impact search-and-rescue operations can have on us. There are times when we feel we've escaped, come out without a scratch, immune to all the pain around the situation. But the memory always lingers; often, it lies hidden beneath the surface, watching and waiting to catch us off guard. Months after the young man's death, Áine was attending another removal following a tragedy when she was unexpectedly introduced to his parents. Her mouth dried, her face flushed, and she dashed off, unable to speak to them. She took some time to compose herself, and returned later to apologise. The empathy she felt was deeper than she ever imagined, but it had lain almost dormant until then, and might never have surfaced had she not come face to face with his parents. She tries to stay detached, to avoid becoming familiar with the personal details surrounding missing persons and their families. It's her way of coping, of keeping her eye on the ball and getting on with the job.

To this very day, the young man's heartbroken mother still phones me just to say thanks again for our help. She believes that there was no way her son could have stood idly by and watched the young couple drown. He had to help. On a working holiday in America only two years earlier, he had also saved the life of a young boy. He was a true, selfless hero, as was the other young man who answered the cries for help on that first, tragic Sunday in September.

Coole Mountain Tragedy

In April 2007 we got the shout. A young Tipperary man had disappeared after a rave party in west Cork. The twenty-five-year-old went missing after he attended a party on Coole Mountain near Dunmanway. There was grave concern for his safety, especially as he was an insulin-dependent diabetic.

A massive search got underway, and focused mainly on the mountainside and forest outside the town. Volunteers came out in their hundreds, and joined forces with the gardaí, Coast Guard, naval divers and a helicopter. The search had been ongoing for several days before Glen Barton and I were called in with the dogs – Lucy the bloodhound and air-scenting Bob. Glen was only starting out in search and rescue, and he came to observe, to get a feel for a real-life search. Training sessions fail to adequately reflect real-life scenarios, and search-dog tests bear very little resemblance to realistic search operations. As training confines searches to specific areas and within certain boundaries, Glen needed to experience the reality of a search for himself, to sense the urgency, feel the drive, get that adrenaline rush, and he had come to Dunmanway as part of the learning process. We began by listening to a briefing.

At 9.30 a.m. on the Sunday after the party, the young man had contacted his family and told them he was lost. He sounded very distressed. Many people in the Dunmanway area said they had sightings of him. One person reported spotting him walking along the road in Moneyreague, about eight miles from the town. A farmer told how he had seen a strange young fellow in his farmyard in the dark of night, and described him as being drenched to the bone. When the farmer approached him, the young man said he was very frightened because he was being chased. The farmer hunted him away, and he thought the stranger had headed off down through the fields. That was actually the last sighting of the missing man.

After the briefing, we set off with a local guide. We had been asked to search with Lucy through the town of Dunmanway, and then to move out from the town on foot to a few locations in which there had been possible sightings. As it was 7 p.m., the town was relatively quiet, but the garda cars and dogs signalled activity. Once the locals became aware of our presence and saw the dogs working, throngs of people appeared from nowhere. Some came out of the pubs with their drinks, stood with their backs to the wall and watched us as we searched. Others gathered in groups, whispering in doorways, following our every move.

Lucy showed her exceptional powers of concentration. She sniffed around the feet of people on the main street and down alleyways, ignoring any distraction around her. She smelled all along the bottom of doorways and up the sides. When we came to a raised bed of flowers, she walked along all the sides of the perimeter; scent can lodge in these holes and hollows. Any time I work with her, I feel like a passenger.

Áine, being Lucy's owner and trainer, understands her much better. Whenever I handle Lucy, she teaches me something new on every search, and moves at such a fast pace that I barely manage to keep up with her. In some ways, working with air-scenting dogs is easier on the handler as they usually work without a lead, can range ahead, and the handlers do not have to follow every step of the way. Normally, bloodhounds are not let loose while searching, but work on a thirty-foot line attached to a harness, which means that everywhere the bloodhounds go the handlers must follow. Any dog can trail, but bloodhounds are better than others because that's the way they're bred. They possess a natural ability to follow scents regardless of what's happening around them. Give them an article to scent, take them to where the missing person was last seen, and they're away.

Our search in Dunmanway that night – in both the town and on roads where there had been possible sightings – yielded nothing. There were no clues. The reported sightings did not stand up. We called it a day, headed for our van, and drove back to Cork. The following day, we resumed the search at 10 a.m. As we were walking out to the farm where the young man was possibly last seen, a Mercedes pulled up beside us with three people inside. One of the Civil Defence guys introduced the car passengers to us as the father, the brother and the sister of the missing man. We spoke together for a few minutes, and our hearts went out to them. Often, once the family of the missing person sees the dogs out searching, they automatically think the dogs will be successful in locating their loved one. We don't ever dishearten them as we always search under the assumption that we are looking for a live person, knowing that the missing person may be lost, injured or suffering from hypothermia. Afterwards, one of the gardaí told me that the young man's father had thought we were being paid to carry out the search; when he discovered otherwise, he said to the garda he would pay us whatever we wanted. The garda said, 'I'd say he'd sell his house.' Needless to say, we do not accept payment as our services are voluntary.

We continued on to the farm, searched around the farmyard, and combed the outbuildings. Then we moved out into the fields and trawled our way through heavy bogland until we came to a river. Three feet deep and flowing fast, it looked highly dangerous, but I thought it could be crossed. More than likely, the young man had waded through it on his way to the farmyard, and crossed it again when he ran down through the fields. But the guide disagreed: he was convinced he would never have made it safely across.

The river flowed through a hollow, and the land around it rose up gradually from the dip to a point where the lights of a few scattered bungalows could be seen. A missing person is always likely to stay near lights: they give a sense of security and direction, and they offer hope, a place of safety. We were heading towards the bungalows when Lucy picked up some scent. She tracked all the way back to the river, and dragged me along with force. Lucy had never been wrong before, and if Áine had been handling her she would have taken charge of the situation and insisted on working the other side of the river. I felt certain that the missing man had paddled through the river on his way to the farm, and had returned the same way when the farmer had become annoyed with him, but our guide was adamant that there was no way the young man would have returned across the river. Generally, I take heed of the local guides as usually they know best. Looking back, I realise I should have insisted, and I regret deeply not following my own instincts and, more importantly, not trusting Lucy.

The land from the farm to the river was marshland, and had no clear pathway. Even if the young man had gone back to the river, it would not have been possible for him to stay on exactly the same trail he had walked along on his way to the farmyard. Lucy was adamant in her indication. The gardaí then decided we should move away and search along a road where there had been another sighting. They have total control over a search and are the legal authority, so I had to follow their instructions. We walked on for a mile down that road, even though we knew that Lucy was likely to pick up any scent within only a hundred yards of the starting point. She found no scent there.

We climbed up Coole Mountain to the site of the rave party. It consisted of a huge, derelict barn with a galvanised roof, a caravan and a makeshift shack. Lucy picked up a definite scent there. We went back down to the roadway. At a fork on the road, we came to a Y-junction and took a right turn. When Lucy found no scent, she doubled back to the junction and searched the road on the left. She seemed to pick up a scent then. We tracked along that road for miles. The gardaí and members of the Civil Defence followed behind us in cars, and there was also a group of volunteers on foot. It was almost midnight when we came to the entrance to a riding school. We were now only two fields away from the river in a straight line. At that point, Lucy appeared to lose the scent.

As Glen and I had to go to work the next morning, we told the gardaí that we would return the following evening if required. When they told us that they were expecting over three hundred people from Tipperary the next day to search, we knew it would be pointless trying to work the dogs with so many people around.

Lucy was lame for two weeks afterwards. She had worked herself so hard in Dunmanway – pulling and tugging me enthusiastically for miles on end – that she had driven her nails back into her feet and was covered in blood. I've never seen any dog work with such concentration and drive.

On the Sunday, exactly one week after the young man had disappeared, searchers found his body just before midday. It was located in woodland at Farranheeny, near the bungalows overlooking the river. The location was less than a mile from where Lucy had indicated, and where a halt to the search had been called for the night. The young Tipperary man had died of hypothermia.

Bandon River Call-out

The shout came from a garda inspector to search for a woman from east Cork. The woman's car had been abandoned near the Bandon river, and the gardaí wanted us to check whether or not she had actually entered the water. On their way to the scene, Áine and Glen stopped off for a briefing at the hall in Innishannon, then headed for Bandon with Lucy. They were joined by Paddy Harkin from Caheragh in west Cork, who owned a young, air-scenting German shepherd named Tara. Midleton Red Cross people were already there; one of their members was related to the missing woman.

Using Lucy, the gardaí wanted to check the woman's direction of travel from her car. Lucy would normally be asked to take scent from the driver's seat, but before doing so, Áine asked the gardaí if anyone had been into the car for any reason. Unfortunately, because of inexperience with search dogs, car seats and other articles belonging to the missing person are usually contaminated by the investigating officers. In this case, Áine was informed that the car had been searched for the woman's mobile phone; regrettably, this compromised the woman's scent. At Áine's request, a relative of the missing woman brought some articles, including a shoe, from the woman's home. A shoe is one of the most likely items not to be contaminated as the inside usually stays untouched by anyone other than the wearer. Lucy took scent from the shoe and quickly tracked from the car to the river bank. Along the way, she stopped at a bush, which suggested that the missing woman may have stopped there for a while. In similar tragedies, I've found that women usually tend to delay their planned actions more than men do. Then, Lucy continued to track on along by the river bank for another few yards. She stopped at the water's edge and gave tongue, indicating to Áine that the woman's final walk ended there. The gardaí now had the information they needed to continue the search. When the inspector arrived, they told him that they were satisfied with Lucy's indication.

The river search was about to begin. Áine and Glen were loading up, preparing to head for home with Lucy, when a concerned relative of the missing woman approached Áine and asked, 'Did she go into the river?' Áine tried to avoid engaging the man in conversation so as to stop herself from becoming emotional. She told him she had spoken to the inspector and he should talk to him. But the relative guessed the answer because he then asked, 'Did she walk far before she went in?'

Later, the body of the missing woman was found in the river. Áine cringed when she was told, and her thoughts were with the missing woman's children. How would they cope without her?

The inspector seemed pleased with the speed of the operation, and the fact that the search was carried out in a low-key manner. The gardaí saw how our dogs worked; they appreciated their value and understood the necessity of calling them in at the earliest stage of a search.

Some weeks later, the Bandon gardaí held a very successful fund-raiser in a local church in support of local charities, including Irish Search Dogs; our members present on the night were introduced to the dignitaries and performers. Those in attendance included the chief superintendent we had met several years previously during the search for the victims of the triple murder in Cork.

For the previous eighteen months, Áine and I, with the help of our club members, had been training up one of our other female bloodhounds. Karla was making great progress and was proving to be an excellent trailing dog. All her training was geared around real-life scenarios. As Karla's primary trainer, Áine decided to offer her to Paddy Harkin. Karla was presented to Paddy in the presence of the local gardaí, who welcomed the additional help in their search for missing persons. Karla continued to be owned by Áine but would be handled by Paddy until one or both retired, after which she would revert to Áine's ownership to live out her life. She is proving to be worth her weight in gold, and is on call in the west Cork area. It is one more step towards pulling all resources together to get to the ultimate goal, which is, of course, finding the missing person.

Puppy Love

Áine and I started Badgershill Kennels to promote the bloodhound as an excellent working show dog. When we decided to put Lucy in pup, we imported semen from an American show champion called Sherick's Flash Fwd at Andorra Kennels; his pet name was Wyley. Lucy gave birth to two pups, one male and one female, making our kennels the first in the Republic of Ireland to breed and work bloodhounds. We kept the female – Cáilín Álainn at Andorra, known as Belle – and gave Watson, the male, to Tom Mulcahy in Midleton, who was a member of Irish Search Dogs. Watson was a large, beautiful, lithe, agile dog, with an excellent temperament and a huge hunger for work, just like his mother Lucy.

Watson and Belle were outgoing and exuberant. They excelled in agility, obedience and trailing. Both dogs contradicted much of the published information on a bloodhound's temperament and response to training. From the beginning, they showed all of the qualities and the work ethic found in border collies and German shepherds, while their off-lead obedience and control matched most of the so-called obedience breeds. When they took their Introductory Search Dog Test, they sailed through it and passed with flying colours.

Watson grew up to be a beautiful dog but died of bloat at

the age of eighteen months. The exact cause of the bloat was not known; we do know that big dogs, like bloodhounds, are prone to twisting their gut and can't be exercised two hours before or after a meal, and must be kept reasonably calm at all times.

Belle was always a great trailing dog – as good as her mother Lucy. In search and rescue, both of them had proved to be as effective as air-scenting dogs, and sometimes more effective, and we wanted to breed on Lucy's lines. When we decided to breed a litter from Belle, Sherry Robertson, the owner of Andorra Kennels, recommended we use Heather's Where Eagles Dare as a sire for the puppies. In lieu of a stud fee, we were to send a puppy of her choice to Lyn Sherman in America.

A dog normally carries pups for sixty-three days, give or take five days before or after that period. In the weeks leading up to the birth, we visited Southview Vets in Clonmel every few days. Sarah and Alan checked out Belle, X-rayed her, felt the movement of the pups and listened to their heartbeat. We knew well in advance that Belle was carrying a large litter, and so preparations for the birth began. As we wanted to keep the pups in the house, we opted to convert one of the box rooms into a large kennel. We covered the floor with plastic, over which we laid plywood. I made a pig bar – a ledge about five inches off the floor and surrounding the four walls – to prevent Belle from accidentally crushing the puppies against the side walls, which were also protected by plywood. The week before their due date, Áine took time off from work and stayed at home, waiting.

Belle was spot on with her timing. The first four pups popped out in only a matter of minutes. We went into a panic at the sight of them, but soon got our act together, took note of their markings, and weighed each one. After the arrival of the first four, we had a lull of a few hours before the next one appeared. In all, Belle gave birth to twelve beautiful pups over a fourteen-hour period.

After the initial weigh-in, we weighed each pup weekly to check up on their feeding progress. We watched them carefully, around the clock. Áine took weeks off work, and I took a week off to help for a while, but it's something Áine loves, and she was the primary carer. We shared the night shifts, and every move the pups or Belle made had us rushing to her to make sure all was well. We relished every second of our time with them, knowing this time was going to be very short but very important.

The hardiest pups quickly stood out from the weakest of the litter, and could be seen fighting their way through for a feeding position under Belle. After only three days, it was easy to pick out individual pups by their behaviour alone. As early as those first few days, tests can be carried out to determine if a pup will make a good working dog (Volhard's Puppy Aptitude Testing is a good guide, and can be accessed at www.volhard.com).

Only a week after the pups were born, poor Belle contracted mastitis, and two of the pups later died despite all our efforts to save them by hand-feeding. They had been the weakest of the litter, and at one stage Belle had rejected them both. She was left with ten pups: six males and four females.

She fed five of them on one side, then the second five on the other. Five were liver and tan, and five were black and tan. Of the ten, four were blankets, which meant that the liver or black colour covered most of their bodies. As their colouring was more unusual than the rest, the blankets would be more in demand with bloodhound purists – the real bloodhound lovers – as pets, not necessarily as show or work dogs.

To give Belle a chance to recover, we fed the pups by bottle with a milk replacement and weaned them at just over four weeks. At one stage, feeding times came round every two hours. That made for a fairly hectic lifestyle, especially as we also had other dogs, including my two certified search dogs, two six-month-old puppies in training, and, of course our three-year-old son Jack. Every morning, we stuck to a 5 a.m. start. We fed the pups, cleaned out the dog runs, put down clean bedding, looked after Jack, grabbed a quick breakfast if we had time, dropped Jack at playschool, and then I headed off to my full-time day job.

We wanted to make sure Belle was comfortable with people coming and going. We welcomed Jack's friends looking at the pups and picking them up. For the pups' sake, this was important, as dogs can become attached to humans very soon after birth – as early as three days old.

Calls came flooding in from all over Europe and America. News of the pups' arrival had spread fast, mainly through American websites and also because the bloodhound community was very small and close-knit. People were ringing not only about the pups but also with the usual doggy problems. One search-dog handler from Spain rang to query our training methods, and asked if he could come to Ireland to train with us for a week. When I explained that our search-and-rescue work was done on a voluntary basis, he couldn't understand why we would provide the service without pay. He tried to pin me down to give him a date for his visit, but I had to defer it as the pups had to be given priority.

We also had a few call-outs for missing people. One night, I headed to Bantry to search for a patient who had gone missing from the local hospital. We failed to find him, and we were told by the medical staff that there was a possibility he had left the country. I arrived back home at 3 a.m. just in time for a two-hour nap before rising again to start the daily routine with the pups.

Keeping all ten of the pups in the house for warmth and to socialise them meant making them familiar with household noises, such as the sound of our voices, the television, and the washing machine as it slowly rotated or spun at speed. Being socialised in this way would help them adjust more easily to their new homes. When I had socialised other dogs, I used to play a tape of very loud or piercing noises – such as the sound of gunshots – so as to teach them to cope with sudden or deafening noises out in the real world. Sometimes, I'd turn up the volume to almost full.

When the bloodhound pups were only three weeks old, I put them into a cardboard box together, placed it in my car with the engine running, and left them there to feel the vibration and hear the noise. Later, I drove them up the village for a couple of hundred yards, parked, and welcomed any passers-by to have a look at them. I believe dogs should be taken out as early as possible. Most owners keep their dogs inside during the critical period of socialisation.

At six weeks of age, we vaccinated all the puppies. After their initial vaccinations, we began to take them out regularly, particularly to the local woods, where they were able to run free and investigate all the strange smells of wild animals, of pine needles, and of humans and their dogs when they happened to walk by. We watched them ramble along, sniff out new smells and climb over briars. They were happy in that environment. People mollycoddle their pups too much instead of taking them out in the critical period of three days to eleven weeks. Pups need to be handled carefully each day by humans. They also need to see and smell other animals, such as sheep and other farm animals. In a pup's life, three to four days is a long time. Humans don't see it that way – we think ahead in terms of years. But dogs change so fast. We need to stop applying human psychology to dogs.

The weeks moved on. Foreign bloodhound breeders were showing great interest in the pups. The phone kept ringing constantly, and e-mails were flying over and back from people who wanted to take a pup. They were all intent on coming to Ireland. We had to book accommodation for their visit and make sure that Badgershill Kennels was in tip-top condition. There was more fuss created over the litter of pups than there was about the Pope's visit to Ireland in 1979! Bloodhound breeders from the US, Finland, Canada, England and Wales began to arrive to have a look at the pups. These are the elite, the golden circle, the people with clout. These well-established, very influential breeders and breed fanciers dictate everything in the bloodhound world (see the appendix).

In one day alone, we parted with five of the pups – all five flew out together to Frankfurt. Then two went on to San Francisco, two went to Los Angeles and one to Helsinki. The house felt almost empty then as we were left with only two pups, Badgershill J. Swift, known as Weeman, and Badgershill S. Beckett, known as Byron. Then one day, a solicitor from Tipperary and his son came to look at the two remaining pups. They had been on the waiting list for two years, and had a choice between Byron and Weeman.

Shortly after the pups were born, Belle had accidentally hurt one of the male pups. When the pups cried, Belle would pace up and down, but once, as she was anxiously pacing over and back, she stood on the foot of one of the males and clipped his nail. From then on, the pup was singled out by Áine for special attention, with plenty of tender loving care thrown in for good measure! Áine called him Weeman, because he was so little. She loved all the pups but had a real soft spot for Weeman. He won her over completely by constantly biting her ear lobe and licking her. On many occasions, I'd find the two of them asleep in bed, and I'd have to take him from her embrace and return him to his mother. Now, as Áine spoke to the solicitor and his son, she wasn't so sure if she could let Weeman go. She wanted to keep him for herself. The son was sitting alone on the couch. Áine was impressed that he was so quiet. She saw Weeman looking at him. Dogs always take to quiet people because they don't pose a threat. Weeman moved nearer to the boy, who picked him up. Áine said to herself: He'll be all right there – okay, that feels right. And she let him go. Áine found out a few months later that the pup didn't eat for two days after leaving her.

Before ever giving birth, Belle had successfully passed her Novice Search Dog Test, which included a minimum of five trails, each three miles long over different types of terrain, such as roads, rivers, bogs and mountainside. All trails were at least twelve hours old and with different starting points, including a scent article, a motor vehicle and a dwelling house. While we know that Belle would make a great search dog, we have decided not to train her any further for now. Instead, we are guarding her like gold as part of our limited breeding programme for better search dogs.

Despite all the demands of caring for and weaning the pups, we intend sometime soon to put Belle in pup again by the same sire – to do it all again one more time so as to produce more top-class search dogs to increase the success rate of search-and-rescue operations.

Badgershill

As Áine and I started Badgershill Kennels to promote the bloodhound as an excellent working show dog, we spend a lot of time training the dogs for active service, and so their mental and physical condition is vital. Unfortunately, when it comes to showing, judges and other show enthusiasts don't appear to agree. According to one or two judges, bloodhounds as show dogs must be as big and heavy as possible. At a recent championship show, one breed specialist said our dogs needed to be much heavier and have more roll. When I explained that our dogs were primarily kept as working dogs, she stated that if we wanted to show dogs then we should keep them in 'show' condition, meaning far too heavy for work! It's such a shame to hear remarks like this, as any working-dog enthusiast knows only too well that in addition to being unhealthy, a heavy, unfit dog is unable to work for long periods of time without tiring. Many of the call-outs Áine and I have been involved in with a bloodhound have lasted up to four days and longer, with the dog expected to work for many hours each day. On average, air-scenting dogs can cover an area of 120 miles during any eight-to-ten-hour working day, and they would be expected to cover this each day for the duration of the search. Trailing dogs, like our bloodhounds, cover eight to ten miles each hour, and more if allowed; this can continue, as with air-scenting dogs, for many days. Provided they have a definite starting point and an uncontaminated scent article, bloodhounds can locate missing persons much faster and more efficiently than air-scenting dogs. But working with bloodhounds can be exhausting for the handlers as they have to walk every step of the way and hold the dogs on lead, which can be very hard on the hands because of the speed at which bloodhounds move and the strength of the pull. Bloodhound handlers usually wear gloves, but they sometimes become so tired and sore that they have to hand the dog over to another handler. In some respects, working with air-scenting dogs is easier.

When show judges examine a working bloodhound – and any dog from a working breed – they should keep in mind the dog's primary function of work. Does the dog look capable of carrying out the job for which it is bred? Is the dog in a fit and work-like condition so as to effectively carry out its task? These are the important questions that show judges should ask. Too much emphasis is placed on beauty points, such as colouring, tail set, ear set and all those other issues brought into judging by people who have most probably never worked a mission-ready dog.

Badgershill Kennels encourages the showing of dogs and continues to press for a balanced, informed and practical approach for assessing a working breed. Before passing judgement, judges should take the time and trouble to learn all they can about the field requirements of a working breed. As well as that, all show dogs from a working breed should have at least a basic working qualification of some sort before being bestowed with the title of show champion.

Since the founding of SARDA in 1987, air-scenting dogs have been used more than any other dogs in search-and-rescue operations in Ireland. The same holds true for every other European country. Now, people are beginning to see the advantages of using bloodhounds instead, and this is one of the reasons why breeding is so important. Neil Powell recently bought a bloodhound-cross from Scotland and e-mailed me afterwards to say, 'Bloodhounds appear to be the way to go!' We offered him one of Belle's litter but he had already made the purchase.

Paddy Harkin, an Irish Search Dogs trainer in west Cork, now handles one of our bloodhounds, An Luan Caoimhe, known as Karla, who was originally bought by us from Sarah Hanford's kennels and then passed on to Paddy. Karla is a daughter of a Marksbury bitch and a Czech dog with the show name Carson Ilvarus of Marksbury. She has many green stars to her credit, and holds the title An Luan Caoimhe Annual Champion 2009, which she won as a one-year-old. She is well on the way to becoming a great trailing search-and-rescue dog.

Recently, many myths surrounding bloodhounds have been dispelled, thanks especially to *MythBusters*, the popular science programme on TV presented by special-effects experts Adam Savage and Jamie Hyneman. For instance, there is a myth that bloodhounds can easily lose a scent if a body enters water – a scenario often enacted in old, black-and-white detective films, where a fugitive's only means of escape proves to be a river. In one episode of *MythBusters*, Adam Savage crossed a river to see if he could cause a trained bloodhound to lose his scent. The bloodhound found him without any bother. When part of Adam's trail was sprayed with pepper, the bloodhound became confused, but only briefly. He soon rediscovered the track and quickly found Adam. Next, Adam washed himself and changed his clothes, and the bloodhound became overwhelmed by his strong scent at the place of washing. The trainer recognised this, and circled the bloodhound widely until it identified the escape trail, which allowed the dog to easily find Adam once again. In another episode, Adam took on the challenge of checking if a person can trick a trained bloodhound by travelling through an urban environment. During the experiment, the bloodhound became overwhelmed by the huge number of distracting smells in the city. Although the dog did not follow Adam's trail, he did succeed in finding him after ninety minutes. The bloodhound handler concluded that a bloodhound experienced in working in cities would be likely to do much better.

In the US, bloodhounds are held in high esteem. Belle's half-sister works with the FBI as an evidence dog. She takes scent from the scene of a crime, and when the suspects are paraded she walks down along the line and indicates. Such an indication stands up as evidence in a US court of law.

Unfortunately, because of all the different agencies involved in searches in Ireland, Lucy is usually only called out a week or two after a person is reported missing, almost as a last resort. What a waste, especially as to date she has six finds to her credit, all confirmed by the gardaí.

The high-profile search for a woman in Waterford shows how our search-dog services fail to be utilised when needed. Shortly after the woman was reported missing in early October

2006, I received a call from the Waterford search team asking me to join the search. Having agreed to take part, I was told I would get another call soon to make arrangements. That call did not come until two weeks later, about thirty minutes after the body was found in the River Suir at Meagher's Quay near Waterford city centre. I was then asked to bring down the dog to Waterford to backtrack from the car to the river. I refused to go, as Lucy should have been called in way before then. She could have tracked from the car to where the body was put into the water, and identified the driver of the car. They had waited until the body was found to call us up; until then, they had used springer dogs from Wales rather than our cadaver-trained dogs. The newspapers were full of the Welsh dogs, claiming that sources said they were the only dogs in the world capable of blood detection. This was rubbish. In other countries, local dogs are called in first, but in Ireland, unfortunately, dogs are usually not called in until very late in the search, by which time the scent has been contaminated.

A similar situation arose when a search took place for a foreign national who was thought to have been murdered in a glen just a field away from our house in Knockraha. I knew the woods and surrounding areas inside out, as well as all the people living there, many of whom were relations of mine. We have trained our dogs in these woods every two weeks since 1983. Any one of our dogs could have combed the entire area efficiently in three or four hours. The authorities may say that there are underlying reasons for not using civilian dogs, but, at the end of the day, there are no rational reasons for not using Irish resources.

In Search of the Missing

In any search, the dogs should always be called in first while the scent is fresh and has not been contaminated. People should be used only as a second resort.

Dog Tales and Sheep

Pat Falvey is renowned for leading the first ever Irish expedition to reach the South Pole, and for climbing the highest peak on every continent. But few may know that he was once involved in the rescue of a sheep that was stranded on a fifty-foot-high ledge in Ballingeary. When Pat was summoned to the rescue by the Kerry Mountain Rescue Team, he phoned me to act as back-up. The farmer had already called in the Macroom fire brigade, but the ledge where the sheep was marooned proved way beyond their reach.

We walked out with the farmer to the area. The land was boggy, with a hill of rock at the centre, on which the sheep was stuck. He stood there, trapped on a grassy, rocky ledge only two feet in width. One slip, one turn, and he was gone. In such situations, rescuers will always try to lower animals down to safety instead of hoisting them upwards. Common sense tells us it's the practical way to go. It's easier and safer. Taking stranded animals up would be impracticable as they would have to be brought back down to ground level again.

Pat and I climbed up 150 feet, about a hundred feet above the sheep. We attached our harnesses, set up the ropes, tied them to each other, and secured them to a rock. My role was to act as belay (fixed point of support) for Pat as he went down. Onto my harness I clipped a figure of eight, through which I would feed the safety rope to Pat. He abseiled down towards the sheep on his own rope, which was separate from the safety rope. The descent was very steep, and the slope was a craggy, mountainous area with huge humps of rock everywhere. Once he reached the sheep, he was able to stand on the ledge. Of course, this was child's play to Pat, who would literally have slept hanging from even smaller ledges thousands of feet above ground.

Pat made a harness with a few slings, which he then tied under the feet and body of the sheep. He clipped a karabiner onto the slings, fastened the karabiner onto his own harness, and lowered the sheep safely down to its anxious owner. We were treated to a cup of tea by the farmer, who also happened to be a maker of blackthorn walking sticks. When I admired them, he very kindly insisted I take one home as a thank-you.

But not all searches for animals have a happy ending for their owners, especially those which involve old dogs. A local woman rang me for help when her Labrador went missing. I knew this woman well because she lived in Blossomgrove, a pretty village near Knockraha, and she ran a performing-arts theatre in Cork city. The Labrador was very old, and I was almost certain that he had gone off to die. But merely as a face-saving exercise and to keep the owner happy, I agreed to search for him. I brought along Dex. He wasn't trained to search for dogs, but one dog will always acknowledge another dog, and I knew Dex would indicate if he came across a dead dog. We spent two days searching around the fields, but with no luck. Soon afterwards, neighbours found the woman's

Labrador lying dead in a garden only half a mile from home. He had settled down there to die. My initial gut feeling was right. Dogs can sense when their time is up. Instinct tells them they must go away, and so they leave their homes to find a place to die. It's a throwback to the original dogs and to older breeds such as gun dogs – to a time when an old dog would be hunted out of the pack and sent away to die. When dogs leave their home to die, they keep on walking until they can go no further. They look for a comfortable place to lie down, even out in the open. They don't necessarily seek a sheltered spot as they know they've come to the end of the road and need only a temporary resting place.

Another time, a young German shepherd stray almost came to the end of his days when he became trapped in a very dangerous position. The Cork Society for the Prevention of Cruelty to Animals (CSPCA) had phoned me to ask if I could help, so I contacted Pat Falvey, who was only too glad to drop everything for another bit of 'adventure'. Pat and I teamed up with the CSPCA inspector on the Lower Glanmire Road in Cork, near where the German shepherd was spotted stranded on the soaring, sandstone cliffs opposite the Ferry Boat Inn, with Montenotte towering overhead.

The dog was caught on a ledge about 120 feet above ground. More than likely, he had plunged from a higher point. The ledge was only a foot wide. If the dog moved as much as an inch, he would plunge to the bottom. For the rescue, we used a dog catchpole, which resembles the handle of a brush. A line feeds through the pole and comes out at the end in a loop. We knew it would be impossible to rescue him unless he stayed completely still. We would have to make him calm.

We made our way up Summerhill – a steep residential street – and went in through one of the houses, and steadily stepped onto the vertical cliffs that overlook the railway track. We were now about fifty feet above the dog. Pat abseiled down nearer the ledge, while I acted as belay above. He had to make sure the German shepherd did not panic or become stressed, as even the slightest movement would mean that the dog would crash instantly to his death. Pat positioned himself parallel with the German shepherd, just a few feet out from him. He didn't make eye contact or put his hand out to rub the dog. Instead, he remained totally still for a few minutes. Then he eased out the catchpole and gently slipped the loop over the dog's neck. Pat was glad the dog showed no resistance as it was the only way he could be saved. Next, Pat used his slings to form a harness for the dog, and carried him safely down. Pat was pictured in the local newspaper hanging off the cliffs on a rope with the dog strapped across his chest, and both of us later received an award for bravery from the CSPCA. A woman from Cobh gave a good home to the stray, whom she named Kerry.

Some years ago, a dog I had bred strayed from his owners in Dublin and ended up in a dog's home in Mountrath, County Laois. The day following the phone call from the manager of the re-homing centre, Áine and I drove up to check out the dog. We immediately fell for him as he had obviously been well socialised with people and children, and also appeared to have had some basic training. We offered to bring the dog home, if necessary, and find a new home for him. The manager said that they would love to find a permanent home for all the dogs in their care but there were just too many dogs for so small a population, and anyone who handed in dogs did so with the understanding that they were likely to be put to sleep. Britain is no different. The UK Dogs Trust 2009 Stray Dog Survey shows that 107,228 stray and abandoned dogs were picked up by local authorities between March 2008 and March 2009. Of those, more than 9,000 were put to sleep. But these figures are just the tip of the iceberg as many other abandoned dogs would have been taken in by rescue shelters, some of them dedicated to certain breeds.

The biggest problem we have in Ireland is not created by most of the pure-bred breeders, but by all those owners of dogs who allow their pets to wander and mate with whatever happens along the way. As I mentioned earlier, issuing a cheaper dog licence for neutered pets on presentation of a vet's certificate confirming that the dog has been neutered, micro-chipped and vaccinated would help control the situation.

Puppy farming is a relatively new business in Ireland, and responsible breeders should not be penalised for the wrongs of a minority. The Green Party has pushed for a law to control breeding. John Gormley's publication of the Dog Breeding Establishments Bill 2009 called for the regulation of dog-breeding establishments. The minister has argued that the bill would safeguard dogs in breeding organisations, assure customers that pups and their mothers would be well treated there and put an end to backstreet operations once and for all. Under the bill, each local authority must have a register of dog-breeding establishments, and the operators must register and pay an annual fee. Hunt clubs, commercial boarding kennels and charitable dog operations such as mountain rescue would be exempted from paying a fee but would be required to register and be subject to a possible inspection. The District Court would have the authority to remove the breeding operator from the register by order, or to subject it to conditions that they may impose. A provision exists for fines not exceeding €5,000 or imprisonment for up to six months for summary offences. These offences include giving false information, failing to display a registration certificate, or obstruction of authorised personnel.

The bill allows existing dog-breeding businesses to continue to operate for three months after the Act comes into force, and proposes that a local authority would not register premises if the application is not in order, if the applicant is in breach of the Act, or if the local authority believes that the premises are unsuitable for the operation of a dog-breeding business. Once registered, each approved applicant would be issued with a registration certificate that must be prominently displayed.

The bill also gives power to a local authority to serve an imprisonment notice on the breeding business if the establishment is believed to be in breach of the Act or if it poses a threat to public health or animal welfare. A local authority would also have the power to issue a closure notice requiring a dog-breeding business to close down.

However, I truly believe any such law will only affect

registered owners. No law will prevent unregistered breeders selling their pups and this proposed law will not protect animals from unscrupulous puppy-farm breeders.

Reminiscence and Recollection

Most searches linger in the mind, even those that ended shortly after they began or never quite got off the ground. Nine out of ten searches are false alarms. When darkness falls and a person fails to return, panic seems to take over and reports of missing persons come flooding in. Many people reported missing usually turn up themselves, safe and well and often unaware they have been reported as 'missing' or that people are searching for them. Before the arrival of mobile phones, I had often driven on a call-out to places as far away as Galway, Wicklow, Donegal or Kerry only to be told on arrival that it was a false alarm. Sometimes, if I was lucky, the gardaí might be on the lookout for me on the road along the way, waiting to tell me to turn back. They knew my van and were often at the county bounds, lying in wait to give me the news that the search was off.

Once, the son of a wealthy business family from County Cork went missing. When his car was found abandoned a week later at the Cliffs of Moher, his mother rang and asked if I would help in the search. I headed off for Clare with Noel Murphy, Richard Cotter, Áine, members of the Midleton Red Cross and the dogs, Zak, Holly, Bob and Lucy.

At the cliffs, we met up with a local farmer, who was a member of the Coast Guard. He very kindly offered to act as our guide as we set about scouring the soaring cliffs, which rise to a maximum of 702 feet just north of O'Brien's Tower. For hours on end, from daytime right through to the evening, we walked the cliffs with the dogs. But they found no scent whatsoever of the missing young man. Later, his mother confided in me that the search had confirmed her belief that her son had simply taken off into the wild blue yonder – probably to Australia – to shake off the shackles of his privileged background and to start afresh. She said he was always getting a slagging from his friends for having been born with a silver spoon in his mouth, and it had never rested easy with him. I never heard if there was ever any contact from him.

Another time, Áine and Lucy rushed to the Macroom area to take part in a major search for a young Traveller girl who was reported missing. The girl had been watching television at home with her mother on a Friday night. She said she was feeling tired and went to bed early. Later, when her brother peeped in to check on her, he found an empty bed. A garda superintendent led the search, which took place around the fields and farms near Macroom. Over one hundred locals took part, along with members of An Garda Síochána and the Civil Defence. A description of the girl was issued stating that she was dressed in navy trousers, brown shoes and a brown hoodie. Locals reported two reliable sightings of her on the Saturday morning. The girl's mother said her daughter's attitude had changed recently, and something seemed to be upsetting her. The gardaí believed the girl might have been trying to make her way to relatives in Dunmanway. As it turned out, the girl wasn't missing at all: she had run away from home with her boyfriend.

On another Friday evening, a major search got underway for a forester from Glengarriff, who had been planting trees at the side of a mountain in Kenmare. He had arranged to be collected at a certain nearby road after work. When he failed to turn up at the meeting point, he was reported missing. However, he had misread his direction and ended up waiting on the wrong road. Once there was no sign of his lift home, he contacted his wife to come for him. Later, while sitting at home in front of the fire watching television, he heard on the news that a search was underway to find him.

On one search, I was combing through the woods in Connemara. When the gardaí discovered the call-out was a false alarm, they forgot to let me know, and headed off home. I was left stranded at the side of the road with the dog until a lorry driver from Cork spotted us and stopped to give us a lift. As you will understand, I wasn't at all happy.

In all my years of searching, one of the most valuable lessons I have learned is never make assumptions about a missing person. We had been called to a hospital at Sarsfield Court in Glanmire, County Cork, to search for a missing patient. Arriving at the hospital whisked me back in time to my early teenage years, as it was here that my older sister Mary worked and lived when she bought me my first guitar and began to put money aside to pay for my music lessons. The hospital, which was only two miles up the road from my parents' house, had also employed two of my other sisters, Eileen and Mac, and they had lived in too. All three girls worked hard, and resided in small, single rooms, though they would return home by bus for a visit as often as they could. Like the three girls, the rest of my family had started work in their early teens, apart from one of my brothers, who became a priest. Now, this felt like pay-back time to the hospital that had given years of employment to my sisters and allowed Mary to pay for my guitar and music lessons. I was here to search for a missing patient and I was going to do everything in my power to find him. The nurses and Civil Defence people had already combed through the buildings and land within the boundaries of the hospital, which was located in a built-up area. The assistant matron told me that some of the patients to have previously gone missing had made their way to the main road and waited for a bus to the city. I brought along Dex and Eiger to work them in turns. While one searched, I kept the other on a lead. If the missing man was in open ground, I knew that the dogs would find him in no time at all. But having scoured the area around the hospital, we found no trace of him.

Then, about a half-mile from the hospital building, we came to an overgrown, gated orchard on rough ground. The orchard was blocked off by ditches and strewn with the remains of old trees. When I suggested that we should search the orchard, I was told not to bother as the nurses believed there was no way the missing patient could have made it down that far because he couldn't even walk to the bathroom without the help of two people. They were so insistent that I gave in and moved on to another area. But I had a gut feeling about that orchard. I knew one of the members of the Civil

Defence well, so later I took her aside on the quiet and asked her to slip in to check the orchard. A few others went with her, and after only a matter of minutes called us in. They had found the missing man there, lying out in the open, alive. He was much more capable than anyone had thought.

The media love a hero-doggy story. Sometimes, they give credit to the dogs even when they don't deserve it! Twenty-three Irish Boy Scouts had been reported missing on the Wicklow Mountains after they failed to return from a day's walk on the hill, which was steep and heavily covered in woodland and heather. On the day, a terrible mist had come down and reduced visibility to the point where a safe descent was impossible. The Scouts had no mobile phones and no way of making contact for help. A massive air-and-land search got underway. The press and television coverage was huge, and the media had a field day with the drama. Some of the newspapers the following morning slated the Scouts for ever setting off on the walk.

Dex and I were among the searchers. While working Dex along the top of a ridge, I found footprints near a fence encircling a large area of woodland, which suggested that the Scouts may have headed back down towards the base. I immediately alerted the search base by two-way radio. This created some excitement among the media, and straight away I received a radio message asking me to confirm the 'find'. I repeated that I had only come across several fresh footprints and hadn't actually seen anyone. Shortly after I spotted the footprints, four other searchers were walking upwards from the bottom when they met the Boy Scouts making their way down. All were safe and well but were whisked off to hospital by ambulance as a precaution. It emerged that the Scouts had taken shelter for the night along a tree line after they weighed up the situation and decided that walking down the mountain in the mist was a risk they should not take. The leaders had done everything by the book, and even got a singsong going to keep up their spirits.

Back at the base, a number of reporters interviewed me about the search. I told it as it happened, and pointed to the four people who had first come across the Scouts. But the morning newspapers told a very different story: one front page featured a picture of a dog named Dex that wasn't Dex at all, and a heading stating that Dex had saved twenty-three Scouts!

River Lee Search

At 1.45 a.m. on Thursday 12 November 2009 a young man parted with his friends at Daunt Square in Cork city after a night out with an Irish-language club. When he failed to turn up at his student accommodation, friends tried to contact him on his mobile phone but could not get in touch with him, as it seemed to be switched off. They started to worry, and reported him missing. The last CCTV sighting of the student showed him walking alone through the gates of Custom House Quay an hour or two after leaving his friends. Naval divers searched a part of the River Lee on the Friday, but the search was hampered by bad weather.

On the night after the teenager disappeared, we got the shout. The gardaí briefed us at Anglesea Street garda station. Having obtained some articles of clothing from the missing person's apartment, we headed for Custom House Quay. It was now around 10 p.m., and the rain was pouring out of the heavens. We needed to answer one question for the gardaí: Where did the missing young man go after he went through the entrance gates?

Áine asked Lucy to take scent from the articles, and even though it was raining heavily, she began to cast around in an attempt to pick up a trail. Lucy – being the wise, experienced old dog that she is – searched every nook and cranny around the entrance gates for scent. She knows that scent will lodge and hold in holes in the ground, pillars and walls, and under wheel arches in parked cars or any sheltered spot in the area. After a few minutes, she picked up and began heading in from the gates. Despite the bad weather, she seemed to be on a definite trail. Having worked bloodhounds for the past several years, we know that Irish weather is not extreme enough to prevent them from trailing successfully. Lucy and the other hounds will follow a trail that is several days old in rain or snow without any apparent problem. She trailed in and turned right, ending on the quay wall facing Kennedy Quay. That was enough for us: we trusted her fully now. We told the gardaí that the missing student had stood on the quay wall where Lucy had come to a halt.

On the Saturday I brought along Zak, a trained cadaver dog for both land and water, with many successful finds to his credit. With the co-operation of the Civil Defence River Rescue Unit – which is always willing and able to help – we began a search of the harbour. As we started to comb the river, the boat slowly zigzagged from one bank to the other, over and back, trying to cover every angle, at times almost static. I concentrated on Zak's body language. Good water-search dogs are calm and focused, not like on land, where their indication can be much more animated and vocal. If dogs are overanxious, constantly whining and pawing the water, they are of little or no use as water-search dogs.

Conditions were extremely rough, but the adrenaline was pumping, and we took little notice of the weather. But then, after the first hour, the wind and chill factors made themselves felt. We were frozen to the bone. I was wearing my survival suit and life jacket, but it was impossible to protect my face completely from the wind. Zak might give only the slightest of indications, maybe just the flick of the ears, which I could miss in the blink of an eye.

We began at Blackrock Castle and searched out towards Glanmire. Then we turned around, glided at a different angle, and trawled down along to Brian Boru Bridge. Scent might only exit from the water for a couple of seconds, and the exit point can vary depending on the wind and whether the tide is coming in or going out. Pinpointing exactly where a body might be is almost impossible as once a scent leaves a body it follows the current. A dog may give an indication at a particular point but the body itself might lie a quarter of a mile from there. The Lee is split into two channels: one goes up by the Clarion Hotel and the other flows under Patrick's Bridge. Searching a normal river is easy, but searching a harbour is much harder because of the depth.

At the time, the MV *Julia*, a ten-deck ship, was undergoing a refit and was berthed near Water Street at Horgan's Quay. About a hundred yards below the vessel were two barges. Zak showed a tickle there, a possible indication. We carried on further, and went out beyond Blackrock Castle. When we came back by the barges, Zak again barked. We now had a definite indication.

On Sunday we went out on the river again, and moved back down towards the barges. Zak barked again at exactly the same point. I told the gardaí he was picking up a cadaver scent there, and explained that the scent was exiting the water in that area. The flood-swollen water was foamy and flowing fast. It was now an ocean of waves with a life of its own. Tree trunks, gas bottles and other debris floated swiftly by. We expected that the body would be further down towards Blackrock Castle, but Zak kept indicating in roughly the same spot.

In the early hours of Thursday 19 November, a second person was reported missing after an eyewitness saw a young man swinging from Christy Ring Bridge, falling in accidentally, and being swept along and beneath a second bridge. At that time, pressure on the Inniscarra dam was increasing relentlessly because of very heavy rain. Until then, the danger of flooding in Cork city was usually associated with incoming tides, but now it was the soaring pressure on the dam that posed the major threat. At that point, rumours were already rife on the streets of Cork that the release of water at the dam had been delayed because of the ongoing search for the young student. At 11.30 a.m. the Electricity Supply Board (ESB) said it would have to increase the release of water from the dam in the next two hours. Water discharge would reach three hundred cubic metres per second, but the people of Cork were assured that the release would pose no threat to their city.

Already, farmers close to the river were becoming more and more alarmed by the force of the water, which quickly gushed through their lands, flooding fields, ditches and dykes. By 9.30 p.m. the Carrigrohane Straight on the edge of Cork city – which boasts the towering County Hall on one side and the five-star Kingsley Hotel on the other – had become impassable. Young farmers arriving on tractors to help couldn't even make it through. Cars were swept away. Later, the Kingsley – which had an underground car park – had to be evacuated. A wall at Grenville Place, near the Mercy Hospital, was on the verge of collapse as the water continued to flow non-stop. The city's water supply was also under threat and pumps were shut down.

Between 9.50 p.m. on Thursday 19 November and 3.50 a.m. on 20 November – a period of six hours – the ESB released 546 cubic metres of water per second from the Inniscarra dam, and the River Lee burst its banks. As Friday morning dawned over Cork city, the full devastation of the night before came to light. Businesses and homes had been ruined. Stories emerged about people in areas such as Grattan Street close to the Mercy Hospital who had been sound asleep in their beds, unaware that their homes were already flooded, only to be awoken by kind neighbours banging on their doors, warning them to get out. The quay wall at Grenville Place had collapsed and forced the nearby Mercy Hospital to close its Accident and Emergency Unit. Many staff at the hospital had to travel to work by boat.

The city's water works were also flooded, while the city's main water-treatment plant on the Lee Road was badly damaged, leaving reservoirs with a seriously insufficient supply of uncontaminated drinking water, which was expected to last for less than two days. Already, many homes in the city were without water, and plans were set in motion for the army to distribute tankers of emergency drinking water to the public.

A crisis-management team was set up to deal with the appalling aftermath, and came together in the incident room at City Hall. It was calculated that when the River Lee burst its banks, it left behind a trail of property devastation estimated at €140.7 million.

The storage area of Glucksman Gallery at University College Cork had been destroyed when water came running through the building. Other buildings on the campus were also flooded, and all lectures were subsequently cancelled until 30 November. Calling off the lectures at the college would help the search as more students would now be free to join those looking for their missing fellow student.

When we resumed, we found a river littered with an accumulation of much of the onshore destruction, some of which had lodged deep under the quay walls. A body could quite easily have become trapped there, hidden beneath the rubble and prevented from rising to the surface. This time, Zak indicated a hundred yards further down than before. The area indicated initially was not yet searched as the divers were still concentrating on another section of the river.

A mist had descended over the Lee, making conditions cold, damp and miserable. It was rough going up towards Patrick's Bridge, and the boat was rocky. We were bobbing around in the tide, swaying from side to side, with only two feet to spare going in under the bridges. We had to lie flat to get below them. At 4 p.m. it rained. Searchers had come out in force that day, and the river was dotted with students from UCC combing the river in kayaks. We stopped and asked them if they had seen anything. Their boats were ideal for the search as kayaks can go anywhere, unlike other boats of limited scope. As we neared Christy Ring Bridge, we turned back because there were too many boats on the water. Unknown to us, family members of the second missing man were standing on the bridge; when they saw us turning around, they became upset, and later the gardaí asked us why we hadn't continued on to Christy Ring Bridge.

The second missing person was a thirty-one-year-old Clareman who had been living in Cork city. He was seen leaving the Crane Lane Bar at about 2.30 a.m. after he had watched the Ireland-versus-France World Cup qualifier with friends. The last sighting of him had been at Christy Ring Bridge, where the eyewitness had seen him fall in and watched him being swept away. Newspaper reports said that a scarf and jacket believed to be his were found on Friday 20 November on Horgan's Quay.

The search for the two young men went on, with garda divers, Naval Service divers, Mallow River Rescue Team, Missing Persons Association and volunteers all taking part. Friends and families of the missing men continued to come out in force, with many of them keeping a constant lookout by walking up and down the river bank.

On the following Tuesday, I took a day off work. A guy from the Shandon Boat Club took us out. He was very good on the water as he picked up straight away on how dogs work. That day, we trawled all the way up to Christy Ring Bridge without meeting anyone else on the water. We combed up and down the river for six hours. Again, Zak indicated close to the same spot as before, but the divers still hadn't got round to searching there as they wanted to complete another area first and their team was small in number. Water search is slow, intensive work. Divers work in darkness and can only feel their way through the water.

After a twelve-day search operation, one of the searchers spotted a body in the river at a point under Kennedy Quay, the area where Lucy had indicated on the very first night of our search for the young student and a hundred yards upriver from where Zak had been indicating. Navy divers came and recovered the body, which was later identified as that of the missing student.

The second young man was still missing, and the trawl through the waters carried on. The Lee Rowing Club continued to provide a base for the search, which was co-ordinated by a friend of the young man. My sister Celine knew the missing man well, and said he was a lovely guy. One day, while we were searching, his family came over to us. His parents took a little consolation from the fact that the dogs were out looking for him because they said he had grown up with a dog in his bed all his life. His sister asked me, 'Will ye keep going?' The family of a missing person should never feel that nobody cares. We never forgot about him. Even if some of our members were only out walking their dogs along the quay, they always kept a close eye on the water.

It's easy for us to empathise with the families of the missing. We always remind ourselves that it could be one of us or one of our own tomorrow. Nobody knows. As it happened, only months after the search in the Lee, a member of our own club was confronted with a terrible tragedy when she had to search with her dog for her mother, who had gone missing in the Waterford area.

We never found the body of the thirty-one-year-old Clareman. He had fallen into the Lee at the centre of the channel, unlike the young student, who had fallen in at the south channel, which is narrower and more likely to trap a body under the quay walls.

The Passing

My father's illness was like a magnet, drawing all our family to his bedside at St Patrick's, a hospital situated high on the hills above Cork city, between St Patrick's Hill and St Luke's. All of my brothers and sisters came in their turn, putting their lives on hold to be with him, recalling happier times, telling him snippets of news, trying to take his mind away from his sickness, doing little things for him, like propping up his pillows or topping up his water.

As he had been a silent man all of his life, we knew he wouldn't be making any demands, not even if he needed something. It wasn't in his nature. And so we kept asking, 'Is there anything I can get you, Dad?'

'I'm all right,' he'd always reply, but still we kept asking. Then, about a month before he died, he said to me, 'I'd love a half-glass of Guinness.' I rushed off to a pub in St Luke's, excited to be able to grant him his wish. I told the barman my story and came back with the stout. The barman must have had a heart of gold because every single day from that day on, without anyone ever asking, he came across to the hospital with a half-glass of Guinness for my father. In all these years, I never did get round to thanking him.

Another day, when my sister leaned over and asked him, 'Is there anything you need, Dad?' he whispered in her ear, 'I'd love a kiss from my daughters.'

My father had grown up in Ballymacandrick as part of a warm, country family, in a home where affection was openly shown with hugs and kisses galore. But ours was a different home. My mother was at the helm and she suppressed any physical demonstrations of fondness. Once, when one of my sisters was very young, she happened to sit on my father's lap. My mother came along and walloped her. None of the girls dared go near my father again. But everything has it roots – the present is always chained to the past. And when my mother in her old age finally told me the reason behind her demeanour, I understood. As a child, she had been abused by a priest. Being exploited in this manner had left its mark on her.

The mother we knew was hard, with no time at all for tenderness. In our home she reigned supreme, ran the house with an iron fist, and flaked the daylights out of us if she saw fit. The abuse she endured had a ripple effect and we all paid the price, with the girls in our family always getting the brunt of her anger, more so than the boys. Since we were children we had always known she had a terrible grudge against priests in general, but now we knew why. But it baffled us as to how she allowed my brother John to join the priesthood. He had been earmarked for the mission at primary school – at about the age of ten – when the priests from the Divine Word Missionaries came to the school, recruiting. By the age of fourteen he was signed up and went off to study at a college in Wales. My mother had to sign a document giving him over to the order, body and soul. We were horrified when she called us together and told us he was no longer part of our family. We did not see him for a few years after that, not until he returned as a grown man, accepting of all that the priesthood had taught him, but still one of us.

I missed him all those years. We'd shared a bedroom with our other two brothers, and the two of us were always debating religion, looking for the flaws in the sermons we'd heard at Mass while sitting at the priests' feet as altar boys. But his departure at such a young age never seemed to bother my mother; she had let him go without any show of emotion or loss. But she mellowed in her final years, and once said to me, 'Wasn't I very hard on ye when ye were young?'

She took great delight in the arrival of our son Jack, always rejoicing at the sight of him, and saying, 'At last I can hold him in my arms and listen to him talk to me in his own babbling way!'

When neighbours speak of my mother, they remember her in glowing terms. They recall her beautiful handwriting – you could call it a kind of calligraphy – and the fact that she wrote in ink with an old-fashioned nib. She knew how to put a letter together, and, like her mother before her, was the village scribe for anyone who wanted to apply for a job or write a letter to a politician. The villagers appear to have no recollection of her as the matriarchal disciplinarian we knew.

All of my four sisters were moved by my father's touching request for a kiss, and saddened at the wasted childhood years in which they would have loved to shower him with affection, to sit on his lap, snuggle up to him, hold on tight, feel safe in his arms, and kiss his kind, bristly, unshaven, handsome face. My sisters came to the hospital and kissed him fondly on the forehead. It may have been contrived in how it came about, but he got his final wish and felt the warmth of their embrace.

When I came back one weekend from a training session in Wicklow, I went straight to the hospital to see my father, who was now in his final hours. A nun was sitting at his bedside with rosary beads in her hands, reciting the rosary aloud, the telltale sign that the end was near. My father was under huge pressure, gasping for breath every thirty seconds. I totally lost it when I saw him suffering. 'What do you think you're doing?' I roared at the nun. 'Why don't you just put the poor man out of his misery?' That's what I would have done if I could. That's what he would have wanted me to do and what I'd want anyone to do for me. What good were prayers to my father when what he needed was an end to his pain? I thought of Bob, my collie-mix: when he was thirteen and no longer capable of long runs, his life became miserable, totally unbearable. He started to whine and cry, day and night. I'd given him a good life, I had to stop his suffering, and so I put him to sleep. While it was upsetting and traumatic, I felt no guilt because he was no longer in pain or distressed. My father wouldn't let a fly suffer. He was a gentle, quiet man all his life. He cared for his dogs and put them to sleep when he knew they were suffering and could not be cured. Now he was struggling with no such relief to be had, fighting to stay on this side of the fence while at the same time trying to climb over. But it was too high. He was in between, and I stood there pulling my hair out, helpless.

When he finally went and left only his sweet memory behind, I saw him patiently carving wood to make a horse and jockey, reading his newspaper as he sat in the shed with the dogs at his feet, and calling to me with a smile in his soft, country voice, 'Mikey! Watch what happens next. Gerard's after whistling.'

Shadows of a Searcher

Some things in life never change, and the woodland around my native Knockraha has always held a certain charm for me, ever since I roamed there as a child with Jessie tagging along at my side. I return there often with the dogs when I want to be alone and far away from the world and all its woes. It's a magical, musical place, a remote haven for birds, badgers, foxes and rabbits. When I stand in the middle of its steep, V-shaped valleys, I find myself shrinking in size, looking around in wonder at the majesty of its ancient, lofty trees and the richness of its rust-coloured foliage.

I stroll with the dogs by its river and listen to the rippling stream as it gushes down the hills from the fields above and glistens in the autumn sun. A low wall runs along the side of the stream, keeping it on course, coaxing it into the waiting river, waving it off on its merry way. I ramble on, pausing with the dogs at an intersection in the river. It was here bombs were made in my grandmother's time. The location was ideal as water was needed for the mixture, and the explosives could be made far away from prying eyes.

The woods are steeped in history. A linen mill was built along the river, to which a public roadway ran from our house. It was also used as a Mass path for the people coming from the Butlerstown area, at the other side of the woods, to the church in Knockraha. I move on down with the dogs and into the glen. As I come close to the Fairy Rock, I stall. A sense of eeriness envelops me because as children we were always warned to stay far away from it. Beside the Fairy Rock, I spot the small opening leading to a cave. My father took me in there once, and we crawled along for a few yards, but it was dark and eerie, so I backed out of it quickly.

The woods always take me back in time, reconnect me to my past and remind me of my roots. I can almost smell those red, rosy apples stored in a timber box in the Caseys' hallway and taste the sugar-coated bread fingers prepared for me by the postmistress, Mrs Long. I can see Mick Mackey's paper model aeroplanes as they twirled on the ceiling and feel the tree trunks beneath my feet as I jumped along with Jessie, from one to the other, to cross the river. I can hear Nana's voice the day she told me Jessie had gone away. I catch sight of my mother as she cycled home from the farms, and sense the excitement as I stood beside my father to watch the ferret hunt out the rabbits from the warren.

More so than any other place on earth, the woods around Knockraha awaken in me an appreciation of life, a life I could so easily have lost in a moment of madness at a time when I thought I was indestructible. When I trained in search and rescue, I used to go out with the dogs in hail, rain or snow. I climbed Carrauntoohil in the worst possible conditions, when even experienced members of the mountain-rescue team wouldn't venture out – they were too wise and practical. I got the greatest buzz from having to literally crawl across Beenkeragh Ridge on my hands and knees because the winds were so strong it wasn't possible to stand up. I used to attach my dogs to me to make sure they weren't blown off the mountain.

Once, when a German tourist went missing on Mount Brandon, I threw caution to the wind and went against all I had been taught in training. At 8 a.m. on that Sunday, Don and I stood at the foot of Mount Brandon with the dogs, Ben and Dex, gearing ourselves up to join the other members of the Kerry Mountain Rescue Team in the search for the missing German tourist – an elderly, experienced mountain climber who knew Mount Brandon well and climbed it every day as part of his holiday routine. Everyone was allocated their search areas, and the decision was taken that Don and I should work separately. Dex and I were combing the Brandon Point area when Dex began to make his way down a very steep, vertical, grassy slope overlooking water. He started to indicate deep down into the cliff face with great conviction. As he worked his way downhill along the grassy edges, he barked so forcefully that he convinced me he was giving a very definite indication. What could I do? The area was treacherous. I was on my own with no back-up. If I went down to investigate, would I be able to climb back up? Should I radio the others for help or risk breaking the searchers' golden rule of always putting your own safety first? The indication was so strong, I couldn't resist going against all I had been taught about keeping yourself safe when searching alone. I felt compelled to take action, and acted on impulse.

I knew I would have to rely heavily on my ice axe – a multipurpose mountaineering tool used for climbing or going down dangerous ground, such as steep, slippery areas covered in snow and ice. The axe can also be used as a means of self-arrest in a downward fall. A rope can be tied around the shaft to create an anchor when the axe is buried pick down. As well as the ice axe, I had slings made from webbing; these could be looped to the ice axe to make an anchor if I needed to hang onto a support structure. I drove the axe as deep as I could into the ground, and tied myself onto it with my sling. Very slowly, I began my descent. I clung on tight to clumps of grass, stepped down a little, then took out the axe and drove it back in again. Repeating this process, I gradually eased my way downwards.

When I had gone down about fifty feet, I heard voices. I could see the bow of a small boat nestled in neatly under the cliffs about four hundred feet below me. Then, just as the boat began to move out from under the overhang, I saw two fishermen. Dex's indication was spot on. But these men had nothing to do with the search; we had not found the missing German. As I tried to climb my way back up, I discovered I was stuck. I realised then the serious risk I had taken, and knew I should never have gone down there. I had neglected to put my own safety above all else. Now the cliffs below looked even more threatening.

It's always safer to work in pairs. Don and I had been split up. We had been given separate areas to search in the belief that we would not do anything stupid. Trust had been placed in us. But I had pushed out the boundaries too far. I had acted impulsively. Now I was paying the price. I could have contacted the guys for help on the walkie-talkie, but pride was at stake here. I couldn't admit my own stupidity.

Which was the safest path to climb? There was only one way to find out. I sent Dex back up the slope, and watched carefully the trail he took all the way upwards, noting the point at which he jumped up onto a tiny ledge. As he reached the top and was on the verge of disappearing from sight, I called him back down. I needed to check if he would use the same path on his return. He came down taking exactly the same route as he had taken on the way up. I sent him back up a second time, just to be sure. Then I was satisfied that the path he had taken was my best hope of climbing safely to the top.

Now I was relying fully on the ice axe to help me climb safely up the steep, slippery slope with its small ledges of grass and rock. My heart was in my mouth with fear. One slip, one wobble, and I was gone. I concentrated with all my might and tried to blank out the image of the four-hundred-foot drop below me. I dug in my axe as hard as I could, lifted each foot carefully, and slotted it in as securely as possible. I took my time, made no move without first locating a shelf for my fingers and feet. I was taking no chances here – none. It was a matter of climbing step by step, taking each and every one at a snail's pace. There was no other way. It seemed like a lifetime, but I got there in the end, and made it safely to the top through sheer perseverance.

Meanwhile, at Mass that Sunday morning in the local church, the priest had asked farmers with land under the mountain to check their farms for the missing tourist. When they went home, one particular farmer and his son noticed grey crows circling and feeding. They knew this signalled a carcass of some sort. The son climbed up a rock face on the mountain and reached the ledge where the crows had gathered. Sure enough, he found the missing German there. He had slipped and fallen to his death.

When the farmer's son tried to get back down, he could not. His father went for help. All the searchers were still on the mountain. We were told by walkie-talkie that the missing man was found and that the farmer's son was now in trouble. I checked my map for the area and headed off on a three-mile trek across the mountain. When I got to the spot, many of the other searchers were already there. The body had been laid out on a stretcher, with the farmer's son among those standing nearby, having been rescued from the ledge by the searchers.

Having said some prayers, we set off in a slow procession, taking it in turns to carry down the remains of a man who had so loved the mountain on which he lost his life. Our thoughts were with his wife, who was waiting for his return back in Cloghane, the village where we had buried Rizzo years before. We were nearing Cloghane when we came across pieces of metal. Being well versed in local history, Con Moriarty immediately identified them as parts of planes used in the Second World War, including a section of a wing. Finding them took me back in time to my grandmother's house in Knockraha when a shower of ammunition came crashing down from the ceiling. But this find did more than simply transport me back to my youth: just like the death of the German tourist, it hammered home to me the fragility of life for all of us, always.

The German had died on the mountain. The farmer's son had got into serious difficulty. I had come close to death, too, and was still shivering at the thought of what might have been. But I never breathed a word to anyone about the danger I had brought upon myself – not then, not for a very long time afterwards. I was too ashamed.

We walked on. Con was still recalling snippets of history, such as the fact that hundreds of years ago local tribesmen imprisoned men in caves under Carrauntoohil, and that people shouldered coffins and walked their animals to the fair over the Windy Road, leaving a pathway at one side of the valley that is visible to this very day. I could hear all that he was saying, but my mind was elsewhere. I was still back on that vertical slope overlooking the water, sweating, struggling to make my way up.

Appendix:
Bloodhounds and Bloodlines

A t the age of two, Belle became an Irish show champion, and in so doing became the first bloodhound champion in Ireland in forty years. She became an annual champion in 2008, so is now titled Irish Champion Cáilín Álainn at Andorra Annual Champion 08.

The bloodhound community is very small and also very strict. Bloodhounds are the most controlled breed I've ever come across. We cannot breed a female dog without going back to the original breeder for a recommendation on a suitable sire. This rule was drawn up to ensure that puppy farming or breeding for money does not happen. Pups can only be sold for a price set by the bloodhound club. We must sign and obey the club's code of ethics. Pups must be given health checks and X-rayed for defects.

In 2009, when Belle gave birth to her pups, breeders arrived from all over the world, among them Eileen Peers from Cilgwri Bloodhounds in Wales and Ruth Avery of Millvery Bloodhounds in England. Sherry Robertson of Andorra Kennels flew over from Prunedale in California, and Lyn Sherman, president of the American Bloodhound Association, also came over. Sherry decided to take a pup – a female Áine had named Princess because she seemed to have an air of royalty about her, the same way Lucy had when she arrived from Sue and Nick's. Sherry knew all the history of Badgershill, and is always impressed by the work we do. She became very emotional when she heard about Lucy's success in Bandon during the search for the missing woman from east Cork, and she and Áine spent hours on the phone crying about the family left behind. She chose the name Badgershill East of Eden. Lyn picked the pup believed at the time to be the best of the litter – Badgershill Muldoon of Heather – although you can never be certain. Heather Whitcomb came from Canada. She is one of the top breeders in both Canada and the US, and reached this level with only one or two litters a year. Her kennels, Heather's Hounds, is very prominent in the bloodhound world. She assessed the pups and chose the ones to give to the Americans as they valued her expertise and had asked her to make the selection. Among the breeders she selected for was Susan La-Croix Hamil, owner of Quiet Creek Kennels and also one of the top breeders in the US. She was given a female pup: Badgershill Lady of Quiet Creek.

One of the litter – a female named Badgershill Rev. Awdry, named after the creator of Thomas the Tank Engine – went to Irene Clewes, another well-known person in the bloodhound world, while Badgershill Keats, known as Henry, was taken by Sarah Tye, also from England. Sue and Nick Wheeler – the breeders from East Sussex who gave Lucy to Áine – took Badgershill Kavanagh of Far Cry, a male pup known as Curruthers, while Antero Holappa from Finland became the owner of Badgershill John B. We've since received clips of John B. trudging happily along through a foot of snow in Finland, and we were sent a glossy magazine, *American Bloodhounds Club Bulletin*, with a two-page spread on the four pups we sent to America.

The pup chosen by Lyn Sherman and believed to be the pick of the litter became an American champion at the age of just eight months. Two other pups in the US – East of Eden and Emily Brontë, owned by Lisa McCall – walked off with prizes at the AKC Eukanuba National Championship 2009, winning first and second in the bloodhound section for six-to-eight-month-old bitches.

Dogs begin a show career by starting out on the bottom rung of the ladder and work their way up to hopefully becoming a champion. To earn an AKC (American Kennel Club) champion title and the right to place the letters CH before their names, they must win fifteen points at AKC dog shows. The AKC – a not-for-profit organisation – is the oldest pure-bred registry in the US. Its show serves as the only all-breed qualifying show in the US for entry into Crufts, which is the world's largest dog show.

At AKC Eukanuba championships, points are won by defeating other dogs of the same sex and breed in classes held especially for non-champions. At every dog show, championship points are awarded to only one male dog and one female dog in each breed. Once dogs have clocked up fifteen points, they earn the title of CH. One of our pups in the US is now only eleven points away from becoming a champion.

If dogs continue to show having earned the CH status, they are often referred to as 'specials', which means that they will compete at the national level against other champions, usually with the aim of reaching a top ranking in their particular breed. Breed points are used to establish a dog's national ranking. All points are recorded by the AKC. The number of points awarded depends on how many dogs are defeated in the dog's own breed, with one point being awarded for each dog defeated. So if a dog defeats thirty dogs to win the title of Best of Breed then that dog earns thirty points.

Acknowledgements

Patricia Ahern

Many people helped bring this book to fruition, and I would like to thank everyone involved.

To the families of missing persons: you were my initial inspiration to write a book of this nature.

To Mick: your passion for dogs and your expertise set you apart, and, combined with your openness, humility, sense of humour and the way in which you empathise with others, make you a writer's dream. Thank you for the privilege of writing the book with you, for sharing your life story, for the endless hours of conversation, and for your patience always.

To Áine: you made a huge contribution to this book, and were more than generous with your time. Thank you especially for your enthusiasm, for all the chat, and constant flow of e-mails.

Thanks also to the following: Irish Search Dogs for bringing Mick to my attention by writing about him in a local newsletter; Mercier Press for publishing the book, and to everybody there, as well as Dominic and Hannah, for their support and hard work; Glen Barton of Glen Barton Photography (Corroy, Church Hill, Carrigaline, County Cork: glenbartonphotography.com) for organising the photography and to everyone who supplied photographs; Suzanne Collings for the beautiful foreword; members of the Slaney Sea and Rescue Team, particularly Harry O'Connor for recollecting one of the saddest periods of search-and-rescue operations in Ireland and Eileen Mullally for her painstaking research; Seán Rodgers of the Irish Coast Guard Killybegs Unit for providing information on the Killybegs Coast and Cliff Service Unit; everyone at Pro Musica and Russell's Music Store for their help in recalling music shops in Cork city in previous decades; my former editor, Maurice Sweeney, for believing in the idea for the book from the start, and for encouraging me to go ahead and write it; my friend Ann Murphy for accompanying me to a doggy-training session at Hop Island.

Thanks also to Guardian News and Media Limited 2002 for permission to use their account of the search of the Slaney in 'Sadness along the Slaney', to the *Irish Examiner* for permission to use their figures concerning the flooding in Cork in 'River Lee Search' and to the German Shepherd Association Ireland for permission to use the account of the dog assessments in 'Cumbria'.

Thanks to my sister Mary Lenihan for her dedicated hours of proofreading and for her recommendations, and my sister Joan Newman for her encouragement; my late parents, Eily (née Rea) and Paddy Murphy, for nurturing my interest in writing at a young age and for giving me my first typewriter; my sons Michael and Brian, and my daughter Fiona, for reading the book as it progressed, and for their suggestions and support; and my husband and best friend, Denis, for walking beside me every step of the way on every route I take.

Thank you all.

Mick McCarthy

To my father, Jack McCarthy, for the love of animals and nature that he instilled in me. My father never understood why people would want to go on 'holidays' when there were so many places within our own country, and our own areas, that most of us have never seen. He always said, 'Know your own country first and then, if you have time, you can spread your wings.' I never saw him lose his temper or become angry at anything or anyone. He appreciated everything, even a little piece of waste timber from which he could carve some animal or bird, or a cup of tea and a boiled egg! He remembered the years when he had nothing but tea and 'point' – a piece of meat that was hung on a wall over the kitchen table, which, when eating 'dinner', he would point his piece of bread at before eating. He swore that he was so hungry he could taste the meat off the bread.

To my mother, Mary Gleeson: for reasons unknown to me, the locals always referred to her as 'Daughter'. She worked hard, she played hard, and she reared us hard. She didn't have time for the nice things in life – she was always working too hard to be nice. However, she loved to play cards and ludo with us when she had the time. She didn't suffer fools easily, and was quick to let people know if they dared to cross her. She mellowed as she got older, but she never lost her sarcastic wit and loved nothing better than 'taking the legs' from under someone who was beginning to get 'above themselves'. She was quick to remind us all that she was our mother, and no matter how old we were, we were never too old to get a 'clip around the ear'. But she was my mother, and when the chips were down, she became my mother again. Thanks Mam.

To Mary Dunlop, founder of the Irish Guide Dogs' Association, and her good friend, Monny Flanagan from Garryvoe. I first saw them give a demonstration of obedience and control work at the Cork Summer Show with their German shepherds, and was totally enthralled. Afterwards, I attended obedience classes run by Mrs D., as she was affectionately known, where I learned so much about dogs. Mrs D. was the original dog whisperer. Monny Flanagan was an out-and-out doggy woman. Outwardly, she was a tough, hard woman, but inside had a heart of gold and an affinity with dogs to match Mrs D.'s. She used to regularly call into my place of work in Maylor Street just to say hello. Her visits were short and sharp. Most of the time, all I would hear was, 'Hello, young fella. How're the dogs? Don't answer, I know you're busy. I'll talk to ye some other time.' And then she was gone! But when we met outside of work, we would talk for hours about dogs. When I became involved in training search-and-rescue dogs, both Mrs D. and Monny were among the very few people to regularly phone me and encourage me to keep going. Some years ago, before she passed away, I phoned Mrs D. to tell her how much I appreciated all the time and knowledge she had given me. She told me how she followed with pride every snippet of news about my exploits with the dogs. It is a phone call I will remember forever.

To Dr Basil Crofts-Greene: I first came in contact with Basil when I purchased my first German shepherd puppy from his kennels in Strancally Castle, Knockanore, County Waterford. Though he lived in a very large castle, he was a thorough gentleman who had time for everyone. His whole life revolved around his beloved German shepherds. He was a member of the Society for the German Shepherd Dog SV – the parent body of the German Shepherd Association (commonly known as SV) – from as far back as 1921. When one considers that the first German shepherd was only registered in 1899, it really shows that he was in at the foundation of the breed. He made more show champions in Ireland and Britain than most dog owners dream about. When I founded our first dog club, Basil was our president, and for many years would come to our twice-weekly training classes, where he would teach us everything he knew. He regularly came to my house in Knockraha, where he would sit for hours talking about his life with dogs. Other times, he invited us to Strancally Castle, where he would show us his library of dog books, which contained every book ever written on the German shepherd. He became my second father, and when on more than one occasion I told him this, he would smile and very gently say, 'Thank you.' He gave us many informative seminars on the German shepherd dog, and a kinder, gentler man it was hard to find.

I miss Mrs D., Monny and Basil almost as much as I miss my father for his gentleness and my mother for her toughness and support.

To John and Marie Buckley: John and Marie were the founders of the German Shepherd Association of Ireland many years ago. Undoubtedly, they revolutionised the breeding and training of German shepherds in Ireland. They introduced the sport of *schutzhund* to Ireland, and encouraged all German shepherd owners to train their dogs to become more sociably acceptable. At that time, German shepherd dogs were starting to gain a 'bad' reputation. Most people bought them as guard dogs, and very few of these people bothered to socialise or train them; consequently, accidents occurred. John and Marie, through their dedication and hard work, changed many people's perception of the German shepherd. They founded training groups all over Ireland and Britain. Every year, they invited over to Ireland the best dog trainers from Germany. They sacrificed most of their adult lives for dogs, particularly the German shepherd, and most of the people involved in training German shepherds in Ireland owe them a debt of gratitude because, without their efforts, the sport of *schutzhund* in Ireland would probably not exist. John has judged dog shows and working trials all over the world for nearly forty years. He has given seminars on all aspects of the German shepherd to the elite of dog trainers in every corner of the globe. John and Marie's advice and support to me over the years were invaluable, and I salute them.

To Neil Powell, undoubtedly the father of search-and-rescue-dog training in Ireland, and respected in all parts of the world as a dog trainer supreme: as with the people mentioned above, Neil ranks with the best, and has forgotten more about search dogs and their training than the rest of us mere mortals will ever learn. Following the founding of SARDA Ireland, Neil gave up every sixth weekend to come down to Wicklow to help and advise us budding search-dog trainers. I remember the regular phone calls with advice and encouragement to keep going even when I felt like giving up. Training a dog to be a mission-ready search dog is a time-consuming and very thankless task. If you're looking for gratitude and monetary reward, then search-dog handling is not for you. Being totally voluntary, it soaks up all your time, money and energy. It most definitely is not a game, and requires total commitment. Neil had the commitment, and gave – and still gives – of his time selflessly. His kindness to me shone through in the search for the missing German Boy Scout in County Donegal. His dog Pepper made the find and yet he wanted us to say that both dogs made the find so I would get some credit. He was, and is, a selfless and honourable man who, more than anyone I have ever met, deserves the highest award for his commitment to searching for missing persons.

To Con Moriarty: Con, you were the leader of the Kerry Mountain Rescue Team when I started, and you were so enthusiastic about using the dogs. When I first met you, I was absolutely astounded. You were tall, with long, dark hair, a straggly beard and exactly what I had perceived a 'mountain man' to look like. You took me out on the mountain, just you and me, and – like my father before – you enthralled me with the history, stories and legends about the mountains all around us. We walked and talked, or, should I say, you walked and I ran. My God! Your pace was a mile a minute, and there were often times when I felt like shouting, 'Stop, I'm knackered!' But I stayed with you because I didn't want to miss a single word. You loved the mountains so much that you would use any excuse to close your shop and go walking, which you did on many occasions when I had a day off work.

To Don Murphy, Tom, Declan, Marie, Celine, and my children, Shane, Michelle and Gemma: I could not have trained my dogs without your help. Don: as my fellow dog handler, you were the best travelling companion one could have. In our sojourns to Britain to train and for assessments, you were the cool and wise head when I was having a bad day with the dogs. Declan and Tom: neither of you once complained about spending your Sundays acting as bodies for us. Marie: while I got all the credit, you were the one who looked after the dogs at home and did all the basic training, from obedience to search work. The house was like a show house, and, as Basil Crofts-Greene once remarked, 'You could eat your dinner off the dogs' runs.' When we went climbing Carrauntoohil, you were always first to the top as you were much fitter and faster than the rest of us. You spent many Sundays hiding out on the mountains, especially under and around Carrauntoohil, in all sorts of weather, from warm summer days to freezing days in January. On many occasions, when my dog eventually found you, you were crying from the cold, and yes, you did complain. God, there were times when, having hidden out for five or six hours in some gully or other on the mountain, you could be heard screaming your head off: 'Are ye so-and-so's coming to find me or not?' Like my mother, you were not afraid to use a few expletives when making your point! I had the easy job – I just handled the dogs – while you did all the work. It goes without saying that

I would never have managed to train a search dog without your help.

To my sister Celine: with Marie, ye both travelled everywhere, being thrown around unceremoniously in the back of Don's van. Whenever we went training on the mountains, you and Marie were there to help. Remember Radio Rock – or the Hag's Chair, as it's known to hillwalkers? You had been hiding under the Hag's Chair for many hours, again on a freezing-cold day, and your hands became so cold you dropped one of our expensive two-way radios. We never managed to locate that radio, and we consequently rechristened the Hag's Chair as Radio Rock.

To Shane, Michelle and Gemma: any one or all three of you were always ready and willing to hide out up in Donoghues' field each day after work so I could give the dogs a few quick 'runaways'. You were constantly out in the front garden putting the dogs over the many agility obstacles that were permanently set up. In fact, Michelle, you did most of the agility training with the dogs for which I took most of the credit. You were also the one who did all the tracking training with our *schutzhund* dogs, and there are times now when training that I wish you were here to shout advice, as your knowledge and ability with dogs is as good as that of anyone I have ever met. Like your mother, you were not afraid to bawl me out if you saw me making a mistake when training, and, believe me, I listened! As a family, you had a lot to put up with as I was rarely there, and instead of me helping you all, ye were the ones helping me. Anyway, maybe we could climb Carrauntoohil together again some day!

To Gary Daly: I say thanks sincerely for getting me back dog training, and as a dog handler I rate you as one of the best. I always say that there are only a handful of people that I've met over the years who I would listen to and take advice from about dogs, and you are one of them.

To Áine's parents, Pat and Ann, and my sister Eileen: a million thanks for all the times you spend looking after Jack and Andrew when Áine and I are away training or on call-outs. While we may get the credit for helping to search for missing persons, none of it would be possible without the backing of our families.

To Áine: Áine, you gave me a new lease of life. I dare not think of where I'd have ended up if you hadn't come along at the right time. You are a true 'doggy woman', and you remind me so much of a young Monny Flanagan, with a love for animals that is unsurpassed. I'm never sure what kind of animal you're likely to bring home next. I'm proud of the foresight you had when you took it upon yourself to import into Ireland the first bloodhound for many years. You trained Lucy with very little help from the rest of us as we were committed to air-scenting dogs, but you proved us all wrong. Lucy, as a trailing dog, has proved with her many finds over the years that bloodhounds have become an invaluable part of search and rescue in Ireland. Her reputation and your kennel Badgershill have become synonymous with top-quality working bloodhounds all over the world.

To Jack and Andrew: I say enjoy your young lives and thanks for the fun and happiness you bring to everyone you meet.

Acknowledgements

To Glen Barton: a million thanks for sticking with search-dog training. There were often times when the only training companions I had were yourself and Mary, and, of course, Dilis. Thanks also Glen for all the time you spent taking and sorting out all the many photographs we had to wade through for this book.

To Kieran Murphy, Paul 'Husky' and Claire, Mark and Suzanne, Paddy, Mary, Annette, Pat 'Springer', Tom 'Dice', Derek and all in Hop Island, my genuine and sincere thanks for making dog training so much fun.

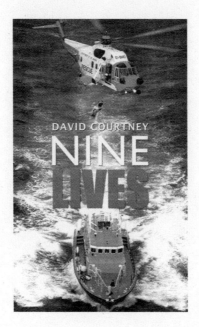

MERCIER PRESS
IRISH PUBLISHER - IRISH STORY

We hope you enjoyed this book.

Since 1944, Mercier Press has published books that have been critically important to Irish life and culture. Books that dealt with subjects that informed readers about Irish scholars, Irish writers, Irish history and Ireland's rich heritage.

We believe in the importance of providing accessible histories and cultural books for all readers and all who are interested in Irish cultural life.

Our website is the best place to find out more information about Mercier, our books, authors, news and the best deals on a wide variety of books. Mercier tracks the best prices for our books online and we seek to offer the best value to our customers, offering free delivery within Ireland.

Sign up on our website or complete and return the form below to receive updates and special offers.

www.mercierpress.ie
www.facebook.com/mercier.press
www.twitter.com/irishpublisher

Name:

Email:

Address:

Mercier Press, Unit 3b, Oak House, Bessboro Rd, Blackrock, Cork, Ireland